THE BOOK OF SAINTS

THE BOOK OF SAINTS

The Lives of the Saints
According to the Liturgical Calendar

Text
VICTOR HOAGLAND, C.P.

Illustrations
GEORGE ANGELINI

THE REGINA PRESS
New York

THE REGINA PRESS
145 Sherwood Avenue
Farmingdale, New York 11735

Copyright © 1986 by The Regina Press
All rights reserved. No part of this book may be reproduced in any
form without permission in writing from the publisher.

ISBN: 0-88271-129-6

Cover and text illustrations by George Angelini.
Text designed and typeset by Roth Advertising.

Source material for this book includes information from *Dictionary of
Saints* by John J. Delaney, © 1980 by John J. Delaney. Doubleday &
Company, Inc., Garden City, N.Y. and *Butler's Lives of the Saints*,
Second Edition, by Herbert J. Thurston, S.J. and Donald Attwater,
© 1956 by Burns & Oates. Christian Classics, Inc., Westminster, Md.

The Regina Press gratefully acknowledges the assistance of Penny Sandoval of the Maryknoll Library, Barbara Curran of Roth Advertising,
Eleanor Eppinger of the Passionist Provincialate, and Julie Crum.

PRINTED IN BELGIUM

CONTENTS

JULY

AUGUST

SEPTEMBER

OCTOBER

DECEMBER

To my mother

FOREWORD

THROUGH THE AGES some people receive a special touch of God's grace. We call them saints. They come from many nations and races. No two of them are alike. Some live into old age; others pass only a few years on earth. Whatever their span of years, their natural abilities or lifework, they are extraordinary human beings who ennoble our human family. The world is better because they have lived.

This book is about saints remembered in the calendar of the Catholic Church. Apostles, martyrs, bishops and missionaries, holy men and women who loved God and his people in a remarkable way. Some died for their faith in Christ; others served the poor, upheld the cause of justice, pursued truth, prayed to God with exceptional results. Like leaven in the earth's mass, they changed the world in which they lived.

The saints lifted the spirits of the men and women of their time who marveled at their likeness to Christ. We today recall them so that our spirits be lifted up too. Their heroic lives inspire us, their love and fidelity challenges us, and their prayers support us. They are companions for our journey of faith.

JANUARY

MARY, THE MOTHER OF GOD

THE CHRISTIAN year begins with a feast in honor of Mary, the Mother of God. First among the saints, she is the loving mother of Jesus and mother of us all.

God chose Mary for a special role in history. She was to give birth to the Messiah, whom God would send to save all people from sin and bring joy and peace to the world. Like a new Eve, Mary became the "Mother of all the living" because her child could bring all generations new life. The prophets of the Old Testament spoke of her in their promise that a virgin would bear a son whose name is Emmanuel, "God with us." And St. Paul would describe her role in this way: "When the fullness of time came, God sent his Son born of woman..."

God prepared Mary with special care and grace. Coming to her home at Nazareth, the Angel Gabriel hailed her as "full of grace," the beloved of the Holy Spirit. Even before her birth God made her holy and free from sin.

Mary's response to the angel reveals her own inner spirit. "Behold the handmaid of the Lord, be it done to me according to your word." Freely and wholeheartedly Mary gave herself to God and committed herself to her son, Jesus, his life and mission.

The intimate union of Jesus and Mary is described in the Gospels. At the angel's visit, Mary conceived her child and in joy hastened to visit her cousin, Elizabeth, whose own child, John, would prepare the Savior's way. With delight Mary showed her newborn son to the shepherds and the Magi as they came to Bethlehem in search of a savior. She presented Jesus in the temple and heard the old man Simeon foretell that a sword of sorrow and contradiction would strike them both. She sorrowed at the loss of Jesus on a pilgrimage to Jerusalem and treasured in her heart his words and the things he did.

When Jesus began his public life, Mary remained at his side. At the marriage feast of Cana, her words of sympathy for the newly married couple prompted his first miracle. She journeyed with him to Calvary and stood faithfully beneath his Cross where, with love and acceptance, she joined in the sacrifice of her dying son. Finally, she accepted the mission Jesus himself would give her in his last moments. Turning to his disciple, John, who represented all of his disciples, Jesus said to her: "Woman, behold your son."

Mary offered a mother's love to the Church that waited for the coming of the Holy Spirit at Pentecost. And when her days on earth were done, she was taken up to heaven to reign among the saints in glory.

Mary still shares in the mission of Jesus, her son. With motherly care she intercedes for those who journey now on earth facing trials and difficulties. She renews faith and love in all who turn their eyes to her.

From the earliest days of the Church till the present, Mary has been honored for the gifts God has given her and the favors she has bestowed on the world. "All generations shall call me blessed, for he who is mighty has done great things to me," she prophesied in her Magnificat. The many feasts of Mary during the year are a sign of her close association in the mysteries of Jesus, as well as the Christian people's love for her over the centuries.

In the days of Advent and the Christmas season, she is frequently recalled for her special role in the birth of Jesus. The Solemnity of Mary, the Mother of God, (January 1) celebrates her place in God's plan of redemption. Two other "Christmas" feasts during the year also honor her: The Annunciation of the Angel Gabriel (March 25) and The Presentation of Jesus in the Temple (February 2).

The Solemnity of the Immaculate Conception (December 8) celebrates the belief that Mary from her conception in the womb of her mother, Ann, was preserved from all stain of original sin. The Solemnity of Mary's Assumption recalls Mary's entrance, body and soul, into heaven.

Mary's birthday is recalled on September 8. Her Presentation to God in the temple is remembered on November 21. The sorrows she endured are memorialized on September 15.

Particular devotions to Mary that have arisen over the centuries are also found in the Church's calendar: the Apparition of Mary at Lourdes in 1858 (February 11), the Feast of the Immaculate Heart of Mary (May 31), the Feast of Our Lady of

Mount Carmel (July 16), and the Feast of the Queenship of Mary (August 22).

Devotion to Mary in the Church is not confined to a single day or a few special feast days. Through daily prayers and acts of piety, such as the Rosary, her memory is constantly evoked throughout the year. Hailed by the angel, "full of grace," she inspires the Church today, as she did the apostles, with a faithful love of her son, Jesus Christ.

> *Loving mother of the Redeemer, gate of heaven, star of the sea, assist your people who have fallen yet strive to rise again. You who received Gabriel's joyful greeting, have pity on us poor sinners.*

ST. BASIL THE GREAT (330-379) January 2 and
ST. GREGORY NAZIANZEN (330-389) bishops and doctors

THESE TWO saints are honored together because they were friends on earth. Schoolmates at Athens, they were baptized on the same day and they both became holy priests and bishops.

St. Basil the Great was born in Caesarea, Cappadocia, Asia Minor in 330. He came from a saintly family that kept the Christian faith through years of terrible persecution. His grandmother, Macrina the Elder; his father and mother, Basil the Elder and Emmelia; his sister, Macrina; and his younger brothers, Gregory of Nyssa and Peter of Sebaste, are all venerated as saints.

He attended schools in Caesarea, Constantinople and Athens. In Athens, Basil formed a deep friendship with Gregory Nazianzen, a fellow classmate.

About 358, Basil founded a monastery by the Iris River in Pontus. He lived there for about five years, praying and studying. While there, he wrote a rule of monastic life based on his experience. Monks and nuns of the Eastern Church today still follow his rule. Basil's monastic rule is to the Eastern Church what St. Benedict's rule was to the Western Church.

Basil was ordained in 363 and became Bishop of Caesarea in 370. He was an eloquent teacher who fearlessly upheld the rights of the Church against the Arian heresy. Arianism denied the divinity of Christ, and many Orthodox Christians were persecuted by Emperor Valens.

Basil died in 379 and is considered one of the great Doctors of the Church.

St. Gregory Nazianzen was of a different temperament than Basil. He was born in Nazianzus, Cappadocia, in 330. His parents, Gregory Nazianzen the Elder and Nonna, are also venerated as saints. After attending school in Athens with Basil, he soon joined him at the monastery in Pontus.

Gregory was sensitive, peace-loving, retiring, and had no taste for the rough political struggles and intrigue that marked the Church of his day.

He was reluctantly ordained a priest by his father in 362, and became the Bishop of Sasima in 372. Gregory, along with Basil, was a staunch defender of the Church against Emperor Valens and the Arian heretics. Upon the death of the emperor, Gregory was named the Bishop of Constantinople in 380.

As Bishop of Constantinople, he was treated with contempt by the majority of his people who were turned against him by jealous rivals. At one point, he had only one small church from which he could speak, but his words and holiness soon became known throughout the Christian world.

In 381, when order had been restored, Gregory retired to Nazianzus where he spent the rest of his years in prayer and reflection. One of the great Doctors of the Church, Gregory died in 389. He is often called "the Theologian" because of his spiritual poetry, his writings on the Trinity, and the eloquence of his sermons.

God hears our requests as if they were for his own benefit. The joy he has giving is more than the joy we have receiving. So ask freely for what you need; but ask only for what is worthy of his goodness.

St. Gregory Nazianzen

ST. ELIZABETH ANN SETON   January 4
(1774-1821)

BORN IN New York City on August 28, 1774, of a prominent Episcopalian family, St. Elizabeth Ann Seton lived during the early years of the American republic and became a foundress of the young, American Catholic Church.

Her father, Richard Bailey, was a distinguished New York physician. From the time of her mother's death when she was three years old, she experienced an uneasy childhood, as shortly afterwards her father remarried and Elizabeth felt neglected by her stepmother.

On January 25, 1794, at the age of nineteen, she married William Seton, a successful New York businessman. Their life together was lively and happy. Five children, two boys and three girls, were born of their union. Elizabeth, friendly and widely popular, enjoyed a busy social life. She was also a fervent member of Trinity Church in New York City, devoting herself to the church's religious and social activities, especially to the care of the poor.

Upon losing his fortune, her husband's health began to fail towards the winter of 1803. Elizabeth sailed with him and her young daughter, Anna, for the warmer climate of Italy to stay with the Filicchi family, with whom they had become friendly through their business affairs. Her husband's condition worsened during the voyage. Unfortunately, when they docked at the port of Leghorn, Italy, they were immediately quarantined in damp, isolated quarters because of a threat of plague. On December 27, 1803, William Seton died there. The young widow and her daughter were released and found a home with the devotedly Catholic Filicchis. "The patience of these dear Filicchis," Elizabeth wrote in her journal. "You would think it was our Savior himself they received in his poor and sick strangers."

As she experienced the faith of this family and the Catholic faith and practices of the people, especially their devotion to the Blessed Sacrament, Elizabeth was drawn to the Catholic Church. Elizabeth returned to New York in May of 1804. On March 14, 1805, she became a Catholic after enduring much struggle within herself and opposition from family and friends.

As a new convert, she enthusiastically embraced her new faith and became a zealous member of a church which then had few members and little social prestige. With the encouragement of other pioneer Catholic leaders, like Archbishop Carroll of Baltimore, she opened the first American Catholic school in Baltimore in 1808 and established a religious community of women, the Sisters of Charity, in Emmitsburg, Maryland, in 1809. Her small community grew and opened schools and orphanages in New York and Philadelphia. Mother Seton has been called the foundress of the Catholic school system in the United States. Today her followers minister throughout the Church in the

United States in schools, hospitals, and various works of charity.

Mother Seton remained a devoted mother to her children and to those women who joined her. Loyal to the Church she loved, she said to her sisters as she lay dying: "Be children of the Church; be children of the Church." Her death occurred on January 4, 1821, and she is buried in Emmitsburg, Maryland.

A few months after she died, her friend and advisor, Father Bruté, wrote to her old friend, Antonio Filicchi:

"Near home we deposited her precious remains on the day following her death. In this little wood she rests with about fifteen sisters and novices who had come to join her. She leaves more than fifty sisters to survive her, to regret her and to follow in her footsteps... She lived only for her sisters and for the performance of her holy duties...

Her distinguishing characteristic was compassion and indulgence for poor sinners. Her charity made her watchful never to speak evil of others... Her special virtues were her attachment to her friends and her gratitude... Her heart was compassionate, religious, lavish of every good in her possession, disinterested in regard to all things."

Elizabeth Ann Seton was beatified on March 17, 1963, and was canonized on September 14, 1975.

She is the first native born North American to be so honored.

> O God,
>> As a little child relies
>> On a care beyond his own,
>> Let me thus with thee abide
>> As my father, guard and guide.

A prayer of Mother Seton

ST. JOHN NEPOMUCENE NEUMANN (1811-1860) bishop   January 5

ST. JOHN NEPOMUCENE NEUMANN was born in Bohemia on March 20, 1811, into a devout Catholic family. He was gifted with a quick mind for study and a rare ability for languages. Desiring to become a priest, he entered his native seminary in 1831. There he heard reports of the desperate situation of the Church in the New World and began to yearn to serve God as a priest in the new American mission. He applied for ordination to various American dioceses, but received no answer from them. Finally, trusting that God wished him to leave his own land for another, he left his family and with about forty dollars in his pocket sailed for New York. He arrived in New York on May 28, 1836. Bishop James Dubois of New York welcomed him and ordained him on June 25, 1836, at old St. Patrick's Cathedral.

Immediately, he sent the young priest to the Buffalo area where a multitude of new Catholic immigrants were settling in small farming communities and towns without any priests to serve them. John Neumann would spend the next four years tirelessly visiting this scattered flock, establishing churches and schools where he could. In his diary he describes his life: "Only a poor priest, one who can endure hardship, can labor here. His duties call him far and near . . . he leads a wandering life. There is no pleasure, except the care of souls . . . the Catholic population is continually increasing . . . many are in extreme poverty. They live in miserable shanties, some with not even a window."

In 1840, John, realizing his own need for spiritual support, decided to enter the Redemptorists. After his novitiate in Pittsburgh and Baltimore, he continued his vigorous missionary life, this time in Maryland and Ohio. He was untiring in his ministry to the growing tide of Catholic immigrants in America, establishing churches, ministering to the sick, preaching the Gospel and strengthening the faith of a growing immigrant population. Above all, he sought to form the young people through catechetical instruction and established Catholic schools to continue to strengthen them in the faith. Two catechisms that he wrote were approved by the American bishops at their first Plenary Council in 1852.

On March 19, 1852, he was appointed Bishop of Philadelphia. In five years, fifty new churches were

built under his direction. Between 1852 and 1860, the number of Catholic schools in Philadelphia increased from two to one hundred. John Neumann's faith, especially his love for the Holy Eucharist and the Mother of God, profoundly influenced his diocese. His strong sense of God's providence, which inspired him to leave his native land, prompted him to undertake great works of faith and service in his adopted nation. On January 5, 1860, he died in Philadelphia of a stroke. He is buried there in St. Peter's Church.

On October 13, 1963, John Nepomucene Neumann was beatified. He was canonized on June 19, 1977, and became the first American bishop to be so honored.

> *Lord,*
> *may your word be truly preached*
> *and truly heard,*
> *and your sacraments faithfully administered*
> *and faithfully received.*

ST. RAYMOND OF PEÑAFORT January 7
(1175-1275) priest

ST. RAYMOND was born at Peñafort, Catalonia, Spain in 1175. His family was very prominent and was allied to the kings of Aragon. He was an exceptional student and taught philosophy at the age of twenty in Barcelona.

In 1210, Raymond left Barcelona and went to Bologna to study canon and civil law. He received his doctorate in 1216 and was made archdeacon by Bishop Berengarius of Barcelona in 1219. In 1222, he entered the newly founded Order of St. Dominic, eight months after the death of its founder.

Pope Gregory IX called Raymond to Rome in 1230, and Raymond became his confessor. Pope Gregory IX also commissioned Raymond to collect and codify the papal decrees which had last been done by Gratian in 1150. Raymond completed this task in about three years, and his work became known as the five books of the 'Decretals.' This study became the cornerstone of canon law for nearly 700 years.

Raymond was named Bishop of Tarragona in 1235, but had to resign because of ill health. He returned to Barcelona and was elected third master general of the Order of St. Dominic in 1238. He revised the Dominican code and resigned in 1240 at the age of 65.

Over the course of the next thirty-five years, Raymond worked and prayed for the conversion of the Moors. He died in Barcelona on January 6, 1275.

> *May the God of peace and love*
> *give our hearts rest*
> *and speed us on our journey;*

guarding us till we come at least
to that vision of peace
where we know only his riches.

St. Raymond

ST. HILARY
(300-368) bishop and doctor

January 13

ST. HILARY was born into a noble and distinguished family in Poitiers, Gaul. He was raised as a pagan, but embraced Christianity after much study of the Bible. Hilary, who was married before his conversion, was elected Bishop of Poitiers about 350.

Almost immediately, Hilary was confronted with the Arian heresy and became a staunch defender of the Church. He was exiled to Phrygia in 356 by Emperor Constantius because of his beliefs and his refusal to become an Arian.

In 360, Hilary was ordered to return to Gaul. Upon his return, he attended the Council of Seleucia and defended the views of the Church, otherwise known as the decrees of Nicaea.

Hilary's eloquent writings, such as *De Trinitae, De Synodis* and *Opus Historicum*, defend the Catholic belief. He died in Poitiers about 368.

Almighty God, Father,
I know that I owe you this:
to serve you always with my thoughts and words.

Your gift of speech to me has no greater purpose
than to be a servant proclaiming you,
revealing to a world that does not know,
that you are the Father of the Only Begotten Son.
St. Hilary

ST. ANTHONY
(250-356) abbot

January 17

ST. ANTHONY was born in the village of Koman, Upper Egypt in 250. He was born into a wealthy Christian family, and when his parents died in 269, he and his sister were left alone.

About six months after his parents' deaths, while in church, he heard the words of the Gospel: "If you will be perfect, go sell all you have, and give to the poor; and come, follow me and you will have treasure in heaven."

Anthony felt as if God were speaking directly to him. He immediately left the church and gave all his property to the poor people of his village. Then, after providing for his sister, he left home to follow Christ.

He chose to live in a deserted place not far from Koman, where he devoted himself to prayer and work with his hands. He gave much of what he earned to the poor and kept only what he needed for his own support.

About 285, Anthony moved and settled on the

top of a mountain where he lived in solitude for nearly twenty years. In the desert Anthony fought one of life's great battles—the battle with oneself. He faced his fears, his disappointments, his weariness, and his sins. Though the devil continually tempted him, Anthony became a stronger person.

About 305, Anthony came down from the mountain and established the first Christian monastery at Fayum. In 311, during the Arian heresy, Anthony went to Alexandria to encourage the faithful. When the persecution abated, he established another monastery at Pispir, near the Nile River. In 312, he returned to a cave on Mt. Kolzim with his disciple, Macarius, and remained there for the rest of his life.

People from all over Egypt and throughout the world heard of this holy man living in the desert. Thousands of them came to his door to see him and ask his advice. Some adopted his life style and many became monks. As a result, Anthony is called the Father of Monasticism.

Everyone who met this shy, quiet man went away with a renewed desire to love God and live their lives joyfully without fear.

In 355, Anthony returned to Alexandria to combat Arianism. He died in 356 on Mt. Kolzim.

God of truth,
may we hear your word,
and do your will.

ST. FABIAN
   (d. 250) pope and martyr
ST. SEBASTIAN
   (d. 288) martyr

ST. FABIAN, according to tradition, was elected Pope in 236 by the Roman Church even though he was a stranger in that city. He condemned Bishop Privatus of Africa for heresy and governed the Church wisely for fourteen years. In 250, he died a martyr during the persecution of Decius. His grave in the cemetery of St. Callistus in Rome still exists, marked by the words, "Fabian, bishop, martyr."

According to tradition, **St. Sebastian** was born at Narbonne, Gaul, and entered the Roman army as a soldier about 283. A devout Christian, he rose to command the emperor's own guards and used the influence of that position to support Christians being persecuted in the city. Emperor Diocletian, discovering his allegiance, had Sebastian tied to a stake and shot by archers. Though left for dead he recovered from his wounds and went to the imperial palace to denounce the emperor's cruelty to Christians. Diocletian then ordered him beaten to death in 288. His body is buried on the Appian Way near the present Basilica of Sebastian in Rome.

Sebastian was venerated as a martyr in Milan as early as the fourth century by St. Ambrose.

Lord, hear the prayers of the martyrs
   and give us courage to witness to you.

(d. 304) virgin and martyr

TOWARD THE end of his reign, Emperor Diocletian, fearful that Christians were causing the gradual decline of the Roman empire, began a general persecution of the Church in the year 303. For about two years, the Christians of Rome lived in fear.

Agnes, born into a wealthy family, was a beautiful young girl of thirteen. She was brought before the Roman governor by some young men who were incensed by her refusal to marry them. They thought the ordeal of a trial would shake her belief in Jesus Christ and bring her over to their sensual style of life.

At first, the judge tried to coax her to renounce her faith by promises of a luxurious and comfortable life. When Agnes remained firm, he tried to terrify her by showing the instruments of torture she would experience if she did not yield. Agnes was then sent to a house of prostitution. Upon her release, she angered the governor when she bravely defended her vow to give herself only to Christ. As a result, he had her executed by the sword. Christians honored this young, defenseless girl for her invincible faith and celebrated her memory by building a great shrine in Rome over the place where she was buried on the Via Nomentana.

The Lord is my shepherd
there is nothing I shall want. Ps. 22

ST. VINCENT
(d. 304) deacon and martyr

ST. VINCENT, a young deacon of Saragossa, Spain, together with his Bishop, Valerius, were sentenced to a lengthy imprisonment for their faith during the persecution of Diocletian in the third century.

After their ordeal, they were brought before Dacian, the Roman governor, who found that Vincent was unbroken in his belief and in high spirits. Soon after, Valerius was exiled.

Infuriated by the young man's resistance, Dacian became obsessed with a desire to subdue him. Using every sadistic torture he could devise, he continually tried to crush the young deacon's resolve, but could not. After Vincent's death, the governor ordered his body hidden in an unknown place, but it was found by Christians who placed it in an honored grave. Vincent died at Valencia in 304.

> *Father,*
> *you gave St. Vincent*
> *courage to endure torture and death.*
> *Strengthen us in your love.*

(1567-1622) bishop and doctor

ST. FRANCIS DE SALES was born on August 21, 1567, at the Château de Sales in the kingdom of Savoy near Geneva, Switzerland. He came from a noble family and even as a child he desired to serve God completely. Though frail and delicate, he had a quick, intelligent mind and a gentle, kind disposition. His family educated him at the best schools of his day.

In 1580, he entered the University of Paris and was drawn to the study of theology. He then attended the University of Padua, where he received his doctorate in law at the age of twenty-four.

His father wanted him to pursue a career in law and politics and enter into an advantageous marriage. But Francis wanted to be a priest. Against his father's wishes he was ordained in 1593 by the Bishop of Geneva.

The Catholic Church at that time was losing many of its people to the new churches of the Protestant Reformation. Francis set out to restore Catholicism in the region around Lake Geneva known as Chablais. Tirelessly and patiently preaching the ancient faith, writing leaflets that clearly explained the Catholic view, he gradually re-established a strong Catholicism in that area. In 1602, he was appointed Bishop of Geneva.

From his residence at Annecy he organized his diocese and with a winning gentleness ministered to his people. His encouragement and wise counsel inspired many people to a better way of life. In 1608, his most famous book, *An Introduction to a Devout Life*, was published and soon circulated throughout the world. In 1610, he founded the Order of Visitation with St.Jane Frances de Chantal, whom he guided in the spiritual life.

Francis de Sales was convinced that God sees humanity as a great and varied garden, each person beautiful in his or her uniqueness. The various callings of life—soldier, prince, widow, married woman—are like the various flowers of the field; God loves them all. Through his or her own calling, each person can find a way to a deeper friendship with his or her creator. Francis approached people with genuine respect and gently guided them to recognize the unique path they would take in life. He made the journey to God joyful and possible for everyone to make. Above all, he advised against despair and the burden of fear.

He died at Lyons on December 28, 1622.

> *Go courageously to do whatever*
> *you are called to do.*
> *Go simply.*
> *If you have any fears, say to your soul:*
> *"The Lord will provide for us."*
> *If your weakness troubles you,*
> *cast yourselves on God, and trust in him.*
> *The apostles were mostly unlearned fishermen,*
> *but God gave them learning enough*

for the work they had to do.
Trust in him, depend on his providence;
   fear nothing.

St. Francis de Sales

THE CONVERSION OF ST. PAUL apostle

THE CHURCH celebrates the conversion of St. Paul because of its extraordinary nature. Paul, who was known as Saul before his conversion, was born at Tarsus in Cilicia, to Jewish parents. A Roman citizen, he was educated in Jerusalem under the tutelage of Gamaliel, a Pharisee. He became a Pharisee and fully embraced the law of Moses. Paul became an avowed enemy of the infant Church and engaged in the persecution of Christians. It is noted that he was present at the stoning death of St. Stephen.

Between the years 34 and 36, Paul was on his way to Damascus to arrest Christians and bring them back to Jerusalem. His encounter with Christ would change his life and have a dramatic effect on Christianity. Paul described to the people of Jerusalem what happened as he set out for Damascus:

"I set out with the intention of bringing the prisoners I would arrest back to Jerusalem for punishment. As I was traveling along, approaching Damascus around noon, a great light from the sky suddenly flashed all about me. I fell to the ground and heard a voice say to me, 'Saul, Saul, why do you persecute me?' I answered, 'Who are you, sir?' He said to me, 'I am Jesus the Nazarene whom you are persecuting.' My companions saw the light but did not hear the voice speaking to me. 'What is it I must do, sir?' I asked, and the Lord replied, 'Get up and go into Damascus. There you will be told about everything you are destined to do.' But since I could not see because of the brilliance of the light, I had to be taken by the hand and led into Damascus by my companions.

"A certain Ananias, a devout observer of the law and well spoken of by all the Jews who lived there, came and stood by me. 'Saul, my brother,' he said, 'recover your sight.' In that instant I regained my sight and looked at him. The next thing he said was, 'The God of our fathers long ago designated you to know his will, to look upon the Just One, and to hear the sound of his voice; before all men you are to be his witness to what you have seen and heard. Why delay, then? Be baptized at once and wash away your sins as you call upon his name.'"

Profoundly influenced by this grace of God, the converted apostle preached Christ to the nations. Today the feast of Paul's conversion ends the Church Unity Octave—an annual eight-day per-

27

iod of prayer for Christian unity. Inspired by Father Paul Wattson, founder of the Society of the Atonement, this observance has spread from the United States to various other lands and is celebrated in many Protestant and Orthodox as well as Catholic Churches.

> Lord,
>> in your mercy
>> and by the power of your Spirit,
>> take away the unhappy divisions
>> that separate Christians,
>> so that we may all be one
>> in faith and love.

ST. TIMOTHY (d. 97) January 26
and
ST. TITUS (first century) bishops

ST. TIMOTHY and St. Titus were co-workers of St. Paul in spreading the Gospel to the Gentile world.

As he is described in Paul's letters, Timothy was young and timid by nature. He was born in Lystra, Asia Minor. His father was Greek; his mother, Eunice, was a devout Jew who instilled in her son a warm, vibrant faith nourished in the Scriptures. Timothy was converted to Christianity by Paul about the year 47. Paul had deep affection for the young man and encouraged him to be unswerving in his ministry. Timothy was with Paul on many of his journeys and was imprisoned with him in Rome. Upon his release, he went to Ephesus and was appointed its first bishop. Tradition reports that Timothy was martyred under Emperor Nerva in 97.

St. Titus was converted by Paul and also was considered to be one of his closest associates. His solid faith, zeal, and capacity for administration prompted Paul to entrust to him the care of a number of churches in Corinth. Titus was ordained Bishop of Crete by Paul and accompanied him to the Council of Jerusalem. About 65, Paul wrote Titus a letter from Macedonia concerning the spiritual administration of the Christian community of Crete. Reportedly, Titus died at Crete at the age of ninety-three.

The Spirit God has given us is no cowardly spirit, but one that makes us strong, loving and wise.

2 Timothy 1

ST. ANGELA MERICI   January 27
(1470-1540) virgin

ST. ANGELA MERICI was born on March 21, 1470, at Desenzano, Lombardy. Both her parents died when she was a small child and Angela drew near to God for support. She was raised by her uncle at

Salo and became a Franciscan tertiary at age thirteen. It was at this time that Angela had a vision stating she would one day organize a community of women.

When Angela was twenty-two, her uncle died. She returned to Desenzano and began to instruct the poorer children in the village in their religion and soon gathered a number of women companions to share her work. Because of her success, Angela was invited to open another school in Brescia, where she was befriended by the nobility.

Angela went to Rome in 1525 and had an audience with Pope Clement VII. He wanted Angela to be in charge of a congregation of nursing sisters, but she declined and returned to Brescia. About 1533, she organized a group of twelve women to help with her ministry. On November 25, 1535, twenty-eight women plus Angela consecrated themselves to the service of God with St. Ursula as their patroness. This is the beginning of the Ursulines, a community of women that has extended worldwide since her death.

Angela was a woman of deep prayer and generous love for the unfortunate. She died at Brescia on January 27, 1540.

Lord, you give light to the world
  through the ministry of St. Angela.
  May our light too shine for all to see.

ST. THOMAS AQUINAS
(1225-1274) priest and doctor

ST. THOMAS AQUINAS, the great medieval Doctor of the Church, was born in the family castle of Rocco Secca in the town of Aquino, Italy, near the great abbey of Monte Cassino in 1225. His father, Landulf, was a nobleman and his mother, Theodora, was of Norman descent. As a boy of five he began his schooling at the Benedictine monastery at Monte Cassino. In 1239, he began studies at the University of Naples. There, Thomas became friendly with the Dominicans and wished to become a member of their community, but his family resisted his wishes. In 1244, his brother led a troop of soldiers and forced him back to the family castle where he was confined for two years. During that time, family members used every method to dissuade him from his goal, but Thomas remained firm, using the time to learn the Scriptures by heart and to study philosophy.

In 1245, his family permitted him to become a Dominican, and Thomas went to Cologne, Germany, to study under St. Albert the Great. His quiet, slow manner caused his companions to call him "the dumb ox," but soon they learned of his genius. "You call him a dumb ox," Albert told his students, "soon his voice will be heard through the world." He was ordained in Cologne about 1251 and encouraged to return to Paris by Albert in 1252. He received his master of theology in 1256.

Thomas became one of the Church's great theologians and thinkers. Upon his return, he taught at the University of Paris. Between 1259 and 1268 he traveled extensively throughout Italy and taught in many of the small towns and villages.

In 1266, Thomas began his famous dissertation, the *Summa Theologica*. He returned to Paris in 1269 and became a confidant of Louis IX. Popes and kings, as well as scholars and students, sought his advice and wisdom.

In 1273 Thomas was unable to complete his masterpiece, the *Summa Theologica*. After a profound experience in prayer, he said to a companion, "All that I have written appears as so much straw compared to the things that have been revealed to me."

Toward the end of his life, someone saw him kneeling before a crucifix, hearing a voice from the cross say: "You have written well of me, Thomas; what reward do you want?" "Nothing but yourself, Lord," Thomas replied.

In 1274, Thomas was summoned by Pope Gregory X to attend the General Council at Lyons to reunite the Greek and Latin Churches. He died on the way at the Cistercian abbey of Fossa Nuova near Terracina, Italy on March 7, 1274. As he received viaticum he prayed:

I am receiving you, my soul's redemption; all my studies, my vigils and my labors are for love of you. I have taught and written much about the sacred body of Jesus Christ. I have taught and written in the faith

of Jesus Christ and of the holy Roman Church, to whose judgment I submit everything.

ST. JOHN BOSCO
(1815-1888) priest

ST. JOHN BOSCO was born at Piedmont, in the diocese of Turin, Italy, in 1815 to a poor farming family. He lost his father at the age of two and was brought up by his mother, Margaret, who struggled hard to provide for her home.

As a young boy of nine he dreamed he was in the midst of a crowd of fighting children, vainly trying to quiet them, when suddenly he heard a woman say to him: "Softly, softly...if you want to win them. Take your shepherd's staff and lead them to pasture." When he awoke John realized his life's work was to help poor boys.

As a young man in his own village, he delighted other youngsters with feats of acrobatics and magic. Then he would lead them to church and speak of God to them.

John entered the seminary at Chieri when he was sixteen; he was ordained in 1841. In 1844, he was appointed chaplain of St. Philomena's Hospice for Girls. Soon after, John resigned and opened a house for poor neglected boys with his mother serving as housekeeper. Throughout the city of Turin

34

he set up residences and schools to teach poor boys grammar and religion and train them as shoemakers, tailors, and printers. By 1856, he had 150 boys in residence and nearly 500 more in oratories throughout Turin. Helping him at this time were ten priests.

Other priests gradually became involved in his work. In 1859, with twenty-two companions, John Bosco formally organized the Salesian Order with the approval of Pope Pius IX. The Salesian membership grew rapidly and soon spread worldwide. In 1872, he founded a community of religious women, Daughters of Our Lady, Help of Christians, to help poor girls. He also founded a third order, the Salesian Cooperators, to assist in his worldwide ministry.

John Bosco genuinely liked the young and all his life avoided any trace of severity with them. "We should see these boys as our own sons," he wrote to a companion. "Be at their service. Don't be overbearing with them. This was how Jesus was with his apostles. He put up with their roughness, their ignorance, and even their unfaithfulness. He treated sinners with such kindness that some were shocked, others scandalized, and others hoped for God's mercy. So he wants us to be gentle and humble of heart."

At his death on January 31, 1888, he left the neglected young people of his time an immense legacy in the many projects and people he inspired. Almost the entire population of Turin attended his funeral in gratitude to him.

God our Father,
  strengthen the young
  in our unsteady world,
  to love what is good
  and rejoice in what is right.

FEBRUARY

PRESENTATION OF JESUS   February 2

FORTY DAYS after his birth, Jesus was presented in the temple by Mary and Joseph to fulfill Jewish law. There he was recognized by Simeon and Anna, who were waiting for the coming Messiah. St. Luke reports the event:

When the day came to purify them according to the law of Moses, the couple brought Jesus up to Jerusalem so that he could be presented to the Lord, for it is written in the law of the Lord, "Every first-born male shall be consecrated to the Lord." They came to offer in sacrifice "a pair of turtledoves or two young pigeons," in accord with the dictate in the law of the Lord.

There lived in Jerusalem at the time a certain man named Simeon. He was just and pious, and awaited the consolation of Israel, and the Holy Spirit was upon him. It was revealed to him by the Holy Spirit that he would not experience death until he had seen the Anointed of the Lord. He came to the temple now, inspired by the Spirit; and when the parents brought in the child Jesus to perform for him the customary ritual of the law, he took him in his arms and blessed God in these words:

"Now, Master, you can dismiss your servant in peace; you have fulfilled your word.

For my eyes have witnessed your saving deed
   displayed for all the peoples to see:
A revealing light to the Gentiles,
   the glory of your people Israel."

This feast, celebrated by the Christian Churches
of East and West at an early date, has also been called
"Candlemas Day" because candles are blessed and
lighted this day on which Simeon called Jesus "a
light to the Gentiles."

*Christ your Son became man for us and was
presented in the temple.*

ST. BLASE   February 3
(d. 316) bishop and martyr

THERE IS no accurate historical evidence about St.
Blase's life. He was born into a wealthy family and
received a Christian education. He was appointed
Bishop of Sebaste in Armenia and was martyred
during the persecution of Licinius by Agricolaus,
Governor of Cappadocia and Lower Armenia, in
316.

According to tradition, Blase retreated to a cave
and became a hermit during the persecution of Licinius. While there, he befriended wild animals and
cared for them when they were wounded or sick.
One day, hunters found Blase in the woods sur-

rounded by wild animals. They captured him with the intention of putting him in prison. On the way to Sebaste, Blase encountered a woman whose little boy was choking to death on a fishbone. Blase healed him and the blessing of throats on this day derives from that story. Blase was then delivered to Governor Agricolaus and beheaded.

Through the intercession of St. Blase may God deliver us from all evils of the throat and from every other evil.

ST. ANSGAR   February 3
(801-865) bishop

ST. ANSGAR, the apostle to the northern European countries of Denmark and Sweden, was born about 801, in Amiens, France. He became a monk at Old Corbie Monastery in Picardy and New Corbie Monastery in Westphalia. About the year 826, he accompanied King Harold to Denmark and worked as a missionary, but returned to France after three years of little success. He was then invited to Sweden by King Björn and succeeded in converting some of the king's court to Christianity. In 831, he was appointed Archbishop of Hamburg. Northmen invaded Hamburg in 845 and destroyed the city. As a result, Denmark and Sweden renounced Christianity.

Ansgar was appointed Bishop of Bremen, Germany, in 848. He returned to Denmark in 854 and continued his efforts to bring Christianity to the fiercely pagan northern countries through a dedicated group of missionaries. He himself converted Erik, King of Jutland, and through his efforts King Olaf of Sweden later became a Christian.

Ansgar wished to preach the Gospel of Jesus even if it meant his death. He died peacefully, however, in Bremen in 865 and is buried in the cathedral there.

> *God of the nations,*
> *may your truth be known*
> *through all the earth.*

ST. AGATHA   February 5
(d. 251) virgin and martyr

ST. AGATHA, according to legend, was born into a wealthy and noble family in Catania, Sicily. During the persecution of Decius, Quintian, a Roman consul, desired her. Agatha refused his advances and was sent to a house of prostitution. She was repeatedly tortured and had her breasts cut off. Subjected to harsh torments, Agatha suffered death with courage and was united to Jesus Christ, her Lord, about 251. On the way to her death she prayed:

Lord my creator,
  you have protected me from birth
  and given me patience in times of trial.
  Now receive my soul.

ST. PAUL MIKI (1562-1597) February 6
and COMPANIONS martyrs

ST. PAUL MIKI was born at Tounucumada, Japan in 1562, and joined the Society of Jesus in 1580. Paul, along with twenty-five other Christians, was executed by crucifixion on February 5, 1597, at Nagasaki, Japan, by officials determined to eradicate the Catholic Church from that country. Three Jesuits: Paul Miki, John Goto and James Kisai; six Franciscans: Peter Baptist, Martin De Aguirre, Francis Blanco, Francis of St. Michael, Philip De Las Casas, and Gonsalo Garcia; and seventeen Japanese laymen, all Franciscan tertiaries, were martyred.

A gifted preacher, Paul spoke his last sermon as he died. He proclaimed himself a good Japanese and a good Christian. "As I come to this moment," he told onlookers, "I tell you plainly that Christianity is the only way to salvation. I pardon my enemies and all who offend me, as my faith instructs me. I gladly pardon the emperor and all who sought my death. I beg them to be baptized and become Christians themselves."

Paul urged the others being executed to be strong in faith. They sang psalms and repeated the names of Jesus and Mary. Finally their executioners killed them one by one with their swords.

For almost two centuries after its founding by St. Francis Xavier in 1549, the Japanese Church suffered severe persecutions. Almost 4,000 Japanese Catholics were put to death during that time. Foreign missionaries and priests were banished from the country, churches were destroyed and religious practices prohibited. Not until the late nineteenth century was the Church able to function freely again.

> God our Father,
>   strength of your saints and martyrs
>   from age to age;
>   give us courage to be loyal
>   until death in professing our faith.

ST. JEROME EMILIANI   February 8
(1481-1537)

BORN IN Venice, Italy, in 1481, St. Jerome served as a soldier in the Venetian army and rose to command the League of Cambrai forces at the mountain fortress of Castelnuovo. He was indifferent to his religion, but while in chains in prison following a military defeat, he turned to God and miraculously escaped to freedom. He resolved to dedicate his life to God and Our Lady, and was ordained to the priesthood in 1518.

Famine and plague struck the Venetian republic and Jerome devoted himself to caring for and educating children orphaned by the disaster. In 1531, he founded orphanages in Brescia, Bergamo and Como. About 1532, Jerome and two other priests founded a congregation of men to care for orphans, named the Clerks Regular of Somascha. Jerome was the first individual to teach children religion by using a catechism. While caring for the sick, he himself caught an infectious disease and died on February 8, 1537.

> God of mercy,
> you gave St. Jerome a merciful heart.
> Help us too to care for the needy.

ST. SCHOLASTICA

February 10

(480-547) virgin

ST. SCHOLASTICA, the sister of St. Benedict, most probably his twin, was born in 480. She followed Benedict when he moved to Monte Cassino and established his own monastery. Scholastica settled nearby in Plombariola and founded a community of women, also believed to be under the direction of Benedict. Scholastica is considered to be the first

Benedictine nun. The only knowledge we have of her is from an incident St. Gregory the Great describes.

She met with her brother once a year, and as she was not allowed in the monastery, Benedict would come to meet her in a home with several of his followers. At their last meeting, sensing that her death was near, Scholastica was anxious to continue their conversation throughout the night and asked Benedict to remain with her to praise God. When Benedict sought to go, Scholastica began to pray, and such a violent storm arose that he could not go out the door. "I asked you a favor and you refused," she said. "I asked it of God and he granted it." Benedict left the next morning. Three days later, Scholastica died and Benedict saw her soul ascending to God like a dove.

Lord, we thank you for hearing
the prayers inspired by our love.

OUR LADY OF LOURDES   February 11

THE VIRGIN MARY appeared to Bernadette Soubirous from a cave near Lourdes, France, in 1858. From February 11 to July 16, the young peasant girl saw "the lady dressed in white" about eighteen times. Mary told her to pray for sinners and to have a church built on that spot. When Bernadette asked her who she was, she replied, "I am the Immaculate Conception." Today the great shrine of Lourdes is a sacred place where pilgrims gather from all the world for prayer, healing, and a renewal of faith.

> *God of mercy,*
> *may the prayers of Mary help us*
> *to rise above our human weakness.*

ST. CYRIL   (825-869)   February 14
monk and
ST. METHODIUS   (826-885) bishop

STS. CYRIL and METHODIUS were brothers born in Thessalonica, Greece. **Cyril,** who was baptized Constantine, assumed the name Cyril when he became a monk shortly before his death. He studied at the Imperial University in Constantinople under Photius. He was ordained soon after and became known as "the Philosopher." His brother, **Methodius,** served as governor of one of the Slav colonies in the Opsikion province. Afterwards he became a monk. In 861, at the request of Emperor Michael II, Cyril and Methodius went on a mission to convert the Khazars in Russia. The two embarked on missionary work that profoundly influenced the Slavic peoples of Eastern Europe.

In 862, Prince Rotislav of Moravia asked the Eastern Emperor for Christian missionaries to teach the Gospel to his people in their own language. Photius, now patriarch of Constantinople, assigned the task to Cyril and Methodius in 863. They prepared liturgical books and later translated the Scriptures into the Slavic language. They also provided an alphabet, known as the glagolithic alphabet, for their writing. Through their preaching and writing they brought Christianity to the countries of Bulgaria, Yugoslavia and Russia.

Emperor Louis the German and missionaries from the Western Church questioned their methods. They sought, and eventually gained the approval of Pope Adrian II for their work. Pope Adrian II ordained them as bishops in 869. Cyril died in Rome on February 14, 869. As he was dying he prayed:

Lord, my God,
  build up your Church and make it one.
  Inspire your people with your words and teaching.
  You called us to preach the Gospel of Christ
    and to encourage them to be pleasing to you.
  I return to you your people, your gift to me.
  Direct them and protect them.
  May they praise you, Father, Son, and
    Holy Spirit. Amen.

His brother, Methodius, continued to labor as a missionary until his death on April 6, 885 in Velehrad, Czechoslovakia.

SEVEN FOUNDERS OF THE ORDER OF SERVITES

February 17

(thirteenth century)

BETWEEN 1225 and 1227 seven prosperous cloth merchants from the city of Florence, Italy, joined the Confraternity of the Blessed Virgin. They were Buonfiglio Monaldo, Alexis Falconieri, Benedict dell'Antella, Bartholomew Amidei, Ricovero Uguccione, Gerardino Sostegni and John Buonagiunta.

On the Feast of the Assumption they were inspired by a vision of Our Lady and began a life of prayer and penance on Monte Senario, a quiet mountain outside Florence. In 1240, their community evolved into a religious community called the Servites which today is found in many countries of the world. The Servites have a special devotion to Mary, the Mother of Sorrows. The Order of Servites was approved by the Holy See in 1304.

Lord, help us to live in peace with others
and share our gifts together.

ST. PETER DAMIAN

February 21

(1007-1072) bishop and doctor

ST. PETER was born into a poor family at Ravenna, Italy, in 1007. He was orphaned at a young age and left to the care of an older brother who mistreated him. Another brother, who was archpriest of Ravenna, became his guardian and had him educated at Faenza and Parma.

Peter became a professor, but left a successful teaching career to enter the Benedictine monastery at Fonte Avellana in 1035. He was elected prior in 1043 and inspired his companions to live an exemplary Christian life. He also founded five other hermitages.

Peter was an advisor to popes and kings, and was appointed Cardinal-Bishop of Ostia by Pope Stephen IX in 1057. His extensive writings were instrumental in reforming the Church of his time. He frequently undertook missions of diplomacy for the papacy to settle disputes and quarrels. Peter also devoted much of his energy to the fight against simony.

Despite his stature as Cardinal-Bishop, Peter wanted to be relieved of his obligations. Pope Alexander II granted him his wish, and Peter retired to his monastery to live a life of solitude. He died in Faenza on February 22, 1072. He is a Doctor of the Church.

> *All-powerful God,*
>   *may we use our gifts, like St. Peter Damian,*
>   *to serve your Son and the people*
>   *for whom he gave his life.*

CHAIR OF ST. PETER   February 22
apostle

IN ANCIENT Rome, families remembered their dead relatives and friends at a feast during the latter part of February in which an empty chair represented their deceased. Since the early Christians did not know the date of St. Peter's death, they remembered him with a feast around his empty chair on February 22. Later, the Church would see the Chair of St. Peter as a symbol of his authority as the first bishop of both Rome and Antioch. It was to Peter that Jesus said, "I have prayed for you, Peter, that your faith may not fail; and when you have turned to me, you must strengthen the faith of your brothers and sisters."

> *Father, you have built your Church*
> *on Peter's confession of faith.*
> *May nothing weaken*
> *your gift of faith and love.*

ST. POLYCARP   February 23
(d. 155) bishop and martyr

ST. POLYCARP was a close disciple of John the Apostle. He was appointed Bishop of Smyrna, and is considered one of the most important leaders of the early Church in Asia Minor. Late in life, he went to Rome to confer with Pope Anicetus about the date of the Easter celebration. This was an important issue in the early Church, and both men decided that the Eastern and Western Churches would celebrate their own Easter.

According to Eusebius, Polycarp was eighty years old when he was betrayed by a servant and seized during the persecution of Christians under Emperor Marcus Aurelius. Polycarp was brought before the proconsul Quadratus. "Disown Christ and I shall release you," the proconsul ordered. "For eighty-six years I have served him," Polycarp replied, "and he has done me no wrong. How can I disown my king who has saved me." Sentenced to be burned on a pyre of wood, Polycarp refused to be bound with nails. "Leave me as I am. He who enables me to endure the fire will enable me to remain on the pyre unmoved." Convinced that his death was joined to the death of Jesus, Polycarp offered this prayer from the midst of the flames:

> Lord, Almighty God,
>> Father of your beloved Son, Jesus Christ,
>> who gives us perfect knowledge of you,
>> God of the angels and all creation,
>> of the whole race of saints
>> who live in your sight!
>
>> I bless you for you have let me drink
>> this day and this hour
>> the cup of your Anointed,
>> and rise to eternal life body and soul,
>> through your immortal Holy Spirit.

MARCH

ST. CASIMIR
(1458-1484)

ST.CASIMIR was born on October 3, 1458, at the royal palace in Cracow, Poland. He was the third of thirteen children of King Casimir IV of Poland and Elizabeth of Austria. Casimir was tutored by John Dlugosz and as a youth developed a deep friendship with God and devotion to Mary. In honor of Our Lady, Casimir frequently recited the Latin hymn, *Omni die dic Mariae,* which is also known as the Hymn of Casimir.

His desire to be poor in spirit like Jesus Christ prompted him to avoid the luxury of court life and its privileges. Instead, he preferred simple food and clothing and devoted his riches and influence to care for the poor people of Poland.

In 1471, his father sent him to lead an army into Hungary to overthrow King Matthias Corvinus. Casimir became convinced before the battle that the war was futile and unjust, so he ordered his soldiers home. Angered at his son, King Casimir IV had him imprisoned at the castle of Dobzki for three months. Casimir served as viceroy of Poland from 1479 to 1483. He had taken a vow of celibacy as a child, and despite pressure from his father, Casimir refused to marry the daughter of Emperor Frederick III.

His integrity, fairness and love for those in need deeply impressed the ruling class of Poland; his people called him "the Peacemaker" and patron of the poor. He died from lung disease at the age of twenty-five on March 4, 1484, and is buried at Vilna, Lithuania. Casimir is the patron of Poland and Lithuania.

> All powerful God,
> by the prayers of St. Casimir
> help us to serve you
> in the cause of peace and justice.

ST. PERPETUA
and
ST. FELICITY (d. 203) martyrs

March 7

THE MARTYRDOM of Sts. Perpetua and Felicity is one of the most moving stories that followed the early persecution of the Church in Africa by the Emperor Severus. **Perpetua** was a noble young woman of twenty-two, the mother of a young child. **Felicity** was her servant, expecting a child to whom she gave birth in her imprisonment. Both were preparing for their baptism when they were arrested and confined to prison. Also arrested with them were three companions: Revocatus, Saturninus, and Secundulus. Perpetua's father, a pagan, urged his daughter to turn away from her faith and go free. Pointing to one of the household utensils, she said to him, "Do you see this vase, father? Can it be anything else? Neither can I ever be anything but a Christian."

Perpetua describes in her diary her first day in prison: "I never knew such darkness. What a day of horror. Terrible heat. Rough treatment from the soldiers. And I was so anxious for my baby! Finally, we were able to get a place in the better part of the prison and I was able to nurse my baby who was hungry."

In a dream she saw a great golden ladder reaching up to heaven, and after being assured she could climb to the top, she saw a tall shepherd surrounded by thousands in white robes. The shepherd said to her, "Welcome, child!" Strengthened by her vision, Perpetua refused to renounce her faith when she was brought before her Roman judge.

Perpetua and Felicity were condemned to die in the arena, consumed by wild beasts before a cheering crowd. During their imprisonment, they so impressed the officer in charge of the prison that he became a Christian, too. Their infants were taken care of by some Christian families, and the two young women walked calmly into the noisy amphitheater. Leopards, wild boars, and bears attacked, but they seemed to escape them unharmed. Calling out to some Christians who were looking on, Perpetua said, "Stand up for your faith and love one another. Don't let our sufferings frighten you." Finally, they were killed by the swords of gladiators. It was March 7, 203.

Father,
Your love gave Perpetua and Felicity the courage to suffer martyrdom.

ST. JOHN OF GOD   March 8
(1495-1550) religious

ST. JOHN was born in Monte Mor il Nuovo, Portugal, in 1495. He enlisted as a soldier in 1522 and served in the wars between France and Spain and in Hungary against the Turks. He gradually gave up the practice of his religion to lead a dissolute life. After the wars were over, he left the army and became a shepherd for a woman near Seville.

When he was about forty years old, he turned to God and decided to give his life to serve the sick and unfortunate. He began to sell religious pictures and books in Gibraltar and opened a religious-goods store in Granada in 1538. After hearing a speech by John of Avila, John suffered a serious breakdown and was confined to a mental hospital. With help from John of Avila, he suddenly recovered and was released in 1539.

With earnings that he made from selling wood, a hospital for the sick and poor was opened in Granada. This was the beginning of the Order of St. John of God. Later on, his devoted assistants would officially organize this religious order. John was a brilliant administrator and a tender nurse of his patients. He soon won the attention of the bishops and nobility of Spain, and they supported him financially.

John fell ill and, worn out from his labors, died on March 8, 1550. He was mourned by the entire city of Granada. St. John of God is the patron of hospitals and nurses.

> *Father,*
>> *grant us love and compassion for others,*
>> *such as St. John of God had.*

ST. FRANCES OF ROME   March 9
(1384-1440) religious

ST. FRANCES was born to a well-to-do Roman family in the Travastere district of Rome in 1384 during a time of upheaval and misery in that city. She married at thirteen to Lorenzo Ponziano, a prominent Roman figure. Their marriage of forty years, which produced two sons and a daughter, was a union blessed by great love and mutual respect.

Frances and her sister-in-law, Vannozza, joined a love for their own families to a life of service to the poor and hungry suffering from the fierce civil wars then disrupting Italy and the Papal States. When plague spread through the crowded city of Rome, Frances sold her jewels and valuables for food for the stricken.

In 1408, her husband's family was impoverished and persecuted during an invasion of antipapal troops led by Ladislaus of Naples. In 1410, Ladislaus again invaded the city and the Ponziano castle was looted and their holdings in the Compagna were burned and destroyed.

From the harsh treatment he received, Lorenzo was a broken man for the rest of his life, sustained only by his wife's loving care. In 1413, Frances' son, Evangelist, died from another plague that spread through the city. Yet, in spite of her burdens, she turned part of her house into a hospital to care for children who were victims of the pestilence. Soon after, her daughter Agnes died.

About the year 1414, the Ponziano family regained their properties and their remaining son, Battista, married a beautiful girl named Mobilia. Her new daughter-in-law had nothing but contempt for Frances, however, and was only reconciled after being nursed by her mother-in-law through a severe illness.

Frances was eagerly sought after for her counsel and comfort by countless Romans who came to admire her character. She gathered other women to care for the needy and about 1426, founded the Oblates of Mary, later known as the Oblates of Tor dé Specchi. Lorenzo died in 1436 and Frances entered the community. She was soon elected as its superior. She died on March 9, 1440, and was revered by great crowds of people who came to honor her from all parts of the city.

Merciful Father,
  help us to serve you faithfully
  in all the situations of our life.

ST. PATRICK   March 17
(385-461) bishop

ST. PATRICK was born about 385 in either Dumbarton on the Clyde or Cumberland to the south of Hadrian's Wall. He was of Roman-British heritage and his father, Calpurnius, was a deacon and a municipal official. He was seized from his father's farm at age sixteen by Irish raiders who sold him into slavery in pagan Ireland. Six years later, he escaped and returned to his home. His captivity, however, had a deep religious effect on him and he longed to bring his Christian faith to the Irish people. In a dream, he heard "the voice of the Irish" calling him back.

Patrick studied at the monastery of Lérins, off the coast of France from 412 to 415. He spent his next fifteen years at Auxerre, France and was probably ordained about 417 by St. Amator.

About 432, Patrick was appointed bishop by Germanus and went to Ireland to succeed Bishop Palladius. He went to the north and west of Ireland where the local Irish leaders welcomed him. Soon he established churches throughout the country and, though opposed fiercely by the pagan Druids,

converted many. In 444, after visiting Rome, Patrick established his episcopal see in Armagh, which became the focal point of the Catholic Church's ministry in Ireland.

Patrick's own account of his conversion and missionary life is known as the *Confessio*. In it he saw himself as a humble instrument in God's hands, given gifts of wisdom and strength to bring an alien people to the true faith. "I am ready to give my life most willingly; to spend myself even to death in this country... Among this people I want to wait for the promise made by Christ in the Gospel, 'They shall come from the east and the west, and sit down with Abraham, Isaac and Jacob'."

Patrick died in 461 at Saul on Strangford Lough. He is the patron of Ireland.

> *I arise today*
> *Through God's strength to pilot me,*
> *God's might to uphold me,*
> *God's wisdom to guide me,*
> *God's eye to look before me,*
> *God's ear to hear me,*
> *God's word to speak for me,*
> *God's hand to guard me,*
> *God's way to lie before me,*
> *God's shield to protect me,*
> *God's host to save me*
> *From snares of devils,*
> *From temptations of vices,*
> *From every one who shall wish me ill,*

Afar and anear,
Alone and in a multitude....

St. Patrick

ST. CYRIL OF JERUSALEM   March 18
(315-386) bishop and doctor

ST. CYRIL was born in 315, raised and educated in Jerusalem. He was ordained by Maximus, Bishop of Jerusalem. He instructed the catechumens for several years and was made Bishop of Jerusalem in 349. At the time, the Church was confronted with the Arian heresy and Cyril staunchly defended the divinity of Christ.

Because of his beliefs, Cyril was expelled from Jerusalem in 357 by Acacius, the Arian Bishop of Caesarea. Cyril went to Tarsus and was reinstated by the Council of Seleucia in 359. In 360, he was again exiled by Acacius, through the intervention of Emperor Constantius, but reinstated by his successor, Emperor Julian, in 361.

Cyril was expelled for a third time in 367 by the Arian Emperor, Valens. He returned to Jerusalem in 378 and remained there for the rest of his life. Cyril and Gregory of Nyssa attended the General Council of Constantinople in 381. At this Council, Cyril accepted the amended version of the Nicene Creed. His great sermons on the Nicene Creed and the sacraments, which survive even today, reveal his deep faith and an ability to teach the mysteries

of Christianity in a way the humblest could understand. Cyril died in 386 and is a Doctor of the
Church.

In baptism you died and were born at the same time.
The saving water was both your tomb and mother.
'There is a time to be born and a time to die,' says the
Scripture, but for you it was the opposite. Your time
to die was also your time to be born.

St. Cyril

ST. JOSEPH   March 19
  (first century) husband of Mary

ST. JOSEPH, husband of Mary and foster father of
Jesus Christ, was a descendant of King David, according to the genealogy presented by the Gospel.
Betrothed to Mary, he decided to divorce her quietly
when he found she was with child, but an angel of
the Lord told him to take her as his wife, since the
child to be born was the "Holy One of God."
  Joseph assisted at the birth of Jesus and became
his support and guide through childhood. In a
dream he was told by an angel to flee from Bethlehem with the infant and his mother, lest Herod kill
the child. He accompanied them to the temple
where Jesus was presented to God. With Mary, he
sought the boy Jesus when he was lost on a pilgrimage to Jerusalem. In his work as a carpenter he

shared the many hours of his trade with his young son.

Joseph, a man of faith, a just man, was a worthy successor to the great patriarchs—Abraham, Issac, and Jacob. He followed the call of God through the mysterious circumstances that surrounded the coming of Jesus. God entrusted this silent, humble man with the unique privilege of raising his only Son as a growing child.

A saint close to God, he is honored as the patron of the universal Church.

> *Remember us, St. Joseph,*
>   *and pray for us to your foster child.*
> *Guard and protect the Church on earth,*
>   *till its time is fulfilled.*

ST. TURIBIUS
OF MONGROVEJO
(1538-1606) bishop

March 23

ST. TURIBIUS was born in Mayorga, Spain, in 1538. He did not intend to become a priest and studied law. He was a brilliant scholar and became professor of law at the University of Salamanca. Eventually, King Philip II appointed him chief judge of the ecclesiastical court of the Inquisition at Granada.

In 1580, over his objections, he was appointed

Archbishop of Lima, Peru, even though he was a layman. He was soon ordained and consecrated and arrived in Lima in 1581. His diocese was a large one and it stretched some 400 miles along the coast of Peru.

Turibius had a serious problem with the attitude of the Spanish conquerors towards the native Indians. In most cases, the clergy were the worst offenders. Turibius fought to restore ecclesiastical discipline and protected the poor from oppression. He established numerous churches, monasteries, and hospitals. In 1591, he established the first seminary in the New World at Lima.

Turibius converted many natives because he took the effort to learn their language, and he visited every corner of his diocese. Sometimes, he would stay two or three days in towns which did not have food or sleeping facilities. It is said that he confirmed Sts. Rose of Lima, Martin De Porres and John Massias. Turibius died on March 23, 1606 in Santa, Peru.

Father,
   through the work of St. Turibius
   you helped your Church to grow in the New World.

THE ANNUNCIATION   March 25

ONE OF the "Christmas feasts" celebrated outside the Christmas season, the feast of the Annunciation recalls the coming of the Angel Gabriel to Mary at Nazareth to announce that she was to be the mother of Jesus. St. Luke records the historic moment:

The Angel Gabriel was sent from God to a town of Galilee named Nazareth, to a virgin betrothed to a man named Joseph, of the house of David. The virgin's name was Mary. Upon arriving, the angel said to her: "Rejoice, O highly favored daughter! The Lord is with you. Blessed are you among women." She was deeply troubled by his words, and wondered what his greeting meant. The angel went on to say to her: "Do not fear, Mary. You have found favor with God. You shall conceive and bear a son and give him the name Jesus. Great will be his dignity and he will be called Son of the Most High. The Lord God will give him the throne of David his father. He will rule over the house of Jacob forever and his reign will be without end."

Mary said to the angel, "How can this be since I do not know man?" The angel answered her: "The Holy Spirit will come upon you and the power of the Most High will overshadow you; hence, the holy offspring to be born will be called Son of God. Know that Elizabeth your kinswoman has conceived a son in her old age; she who was thought to be sterile is now in her sixth month, for nothing is impossible with God."

Mary said: "I am the maidservant of the Lord. Let it be done to me as you say." With that the angel left her.

Luke 1, 28-38

The feast of the Annunciation is an ancient feast of the Church. March 25, the time of the spring equinox, was seen as a significant day by the early Christians who regarded it as the day the world was created, the day of Christ's conception in Mary's womb, and the day of his death on the Cross.

God our Father,
Your Word became man and was born of the
Virgin Mary

APRIL

ST. FRANCIS OF PAOLA   April 2
(1416-1507) hermit

ST. FRANCIS was born about the year 1416 in the town of Paola in sourthern Italy. Devoted to his patron, St. Francis of Assisi, he lived humbly and simply. He was educated by the Franciscans at San Marco and went to live as a hermit in a cave at the age of fifteen. Five years later, in 1436, two companions joined him. This date is believed to be the origin of his religious community of men known as the Minims. The community was officially recognized by Rome in 1474 and called the Hermits of St. Francis. In 1492, they changed their name to the Minim Friars. Francis impressed not only his neighbors, but also kings and high officials because of his simple wisdom and his ability to read the human heart.

In 1481, Pope Sixtus IV summoned Francis to France to see if he could cure King Louis XI, who was seriously ill. Though King Louis XI died, Francis made a profound impression on Charles VIII, the king's son. Charles became both a friend and benefactor of Francis and had monasteries built in France and Rome for the Minims. Francis died at Plessis, France, on Good Friday at the age of ninety-one. The year was 1507.

> *Lord, you give wisdom to the simple,*
> *and make the merest child wise.*
> *Give me the reward you promise*
> *to the humble.*

ST. ISIDORE

(560-636) bishop and doctor

ST. ISIDORE was born at Cartagena in 560. Two brothers, Leander and Fulgentius, and a sister, Florentina, are also venerated as saints. He was educated by Leander and about 600, succeeded him as Bishop of Seville.

Isidore is considered one of the great figures of Spanish history. During his lifetime he devoted much of his efforts to the conversion of the Arian Visigoths who had invaded his country. A man of brilliant intelligence and wide learning, he wrote an encyclopedia called the *Etymologies*, dictionaries, works of astronomy, geography, history and theology. He reorganized the Spanish Church and created an advanced educational system that made Spain a center of culture in Europe.

As Bishop of Seville he governed the Church wisely and enlisted the support of his people through the numerous councils and convocations he attended: the Second Council of Seville in 619 and the Fourth Council of Toledo in 633. At the same time, his house was always crowded with the poor seeking his generous help. One of his last acts before death was to give the poor all that he possessed. Isidore died on April 4, 636, and was declared a Doctor of the Church in 1722.

> *Lord, every tree is known for its fruits.*
> *Let me give from my heart the good things*
> *you have given to me.*

ST. VINCENT FERRER April 5
  (1350-1419) priest

ST. VINCENT was born at Valencia, Spain, in 1350.
He joined the Dominicans in 1367, received further education in Barcelona and Toulouse, and became known as a famous preacher. Vincent became heavily involved in the "great schism," when
rival Popes were reigning in Rome and Avignon
from 1378 to 1409.

In 1379, Vincent became a member of the court
of Cardinal Peter de Luna, who was a supporter of
Clement VII of Avignon. When Clement died, Cardinal Peter de Luna was named his successor and
became known as Benedict XIII. After his election,
Vincent was summoned to Avignon in 1394 and became Benedict's confessor. At first, Vincent
strongly believed that the seat of the Church was in
Avignon. However, he had a vision which changed
his life and convinced him that Benedict's reign
was only hurting the Church.

In 1399, Benedict gave Vincent permission to
leave Avignon for the purpose of preaching. As a
preacher of the Gospel, he moved the hearts and
stirred the minds of people throughout Europe, as
well as Spain. According to witnesses, his words,
eloquent and simple, spoken from a loving convic-
tion, were understood by everyone he addressed,
even though they spoke a different language. Great
crowds flocked to hear him speak of Christ's judgment, and those who listened were moved to

change their lives and turn from their sins.

In 1414, the Council of Constance demanded that Benedict XIII resign his papacy in order to unify the Church, but Benedict refused. In 1416, Vincent advised King Ferdinand of Aragon to withdraw his support of Benedict. When this happened, Benedict XIII was deposed and the "great schism" had ended. Vincent died three years later in 1419, while preaching in France during Holy Week.

If you really want to help the soul of your neighbor, first approach God with all your heart and ask him to fill you with love. Then you can accomplish all you desire.

St. Vincent

ST. JOHN BAPTIST   April 7
DE LA SALLE   (1651-1719) priest

THE FOUNDER of the Christian Brothers was born at Rheims, France, on April 30, 1651, into a very wealthy and noble family. St. John entered St. Sulpice Seminary in Paris in 1670 and was ordained to the priesthood in 1678.

In 1679, he met Adrian Nyel, a layman, in Rheims, and began to work for the education of poor boys. In 1684, he gave all his wealth to the poor and spent much of his effort training teachers. As a result of this, he also gave up his canonry.

Soon after, John founded a community of brothers called the Brothers of the Christian Schools. His methods of education revolutionized the educational system of his time. He founded training colleges for teachers at Rheims in 1687, Paris in 1699, and Saint-Denis in 1709. The schools he founded multiplied throughout France in cities such as Paris, Avignon, Calais, and others. Eventually, schools would be opened all over the world.

About 1695, John formulated a set of rules for his community and wrote his own treatise about education entitled *The Conduct of Christian Schools*. John Baptist de la Salle suffered many trials during his arduous work. It should be noted that the Christian Brothers have become the largest teaching order in the Church. He died on Good Friday, April 7, 1719 at Rouen, France.

> *Lord Jesus,*
> > *you taught your disciples*
> > *to welcome little children.*
>
> > *Bless our youth and bring*
> > *them closer to you.*

ST. STANISLAUS April 11
(1030-1097) bishop and martyr

ST. STANISLAUS was born at Szczepanow, Poland, on July 26, 1030, into a wealthy and noble family. He was educated at Gnesen and ordained to the priesthood by Lampert Zula, Bishop of Cracow. In 1072, Stanislaus became Bishop of Cracow. He was the popular choice of both the people and his predecessor, Bishop Lampert. They revered him for his holiness and priestly devotion to the poor. As bishop, he continued to teach the message of Christ and generously served those in need.

Poland then was ruled by King Boleslaus II, a man whose sensual and cruel tendencies caused great harm to his nation. Stanislaus repeatedly admonished the ruler about his wrongdoing, until finally he excommunicated him from the Church. Enraged by the action, Boleslaus entered the chapel of St. Michael outside Cracow, where the bishop was celebrating Mass and killed him with his own sword. Boleslaus had the body dismembered and sought to hide it, but the saint's relics were recovered and placed in veneration at the cathedral in Cracow. Stanislaus died in 1097.

Lord, keep us strong and loyal to our faith,
and protect those who proclaim your word.

ST. MARTIN I

(d. 656) pope and martyr

ST. MARTIN I was born in Italy. Pope Theodore I died in 649 and Martin was elected to succeed him. As Bishop of Rome, he staunchly defended the Catholic faith against the heresy of Monothelitism, which denied that Christ had both a human and a divine will.

Soon after his election, Martin convened a council at the Lateran and condemned Monothelitism, its leaders, especially Byzantine Emperor Constans II, and two imperial decrees supporting the heresy.

Upon hearing this, Constans became enraged and demanded that Martin be brought before him in Constantinople. Constans then sent Theodore Calliopas and his troops to Rome. Martin was captured, brought back to Constantinople and imprisoned in 653. While in prison, he was subjected to many indignities and tortured unmercifully. After three months, Martin was condemned to death and sent back to prison. His life was spared by the Patriarch of Constantinople, but Martin was exiled to the Crimea where he died in 656.

The Lord himself will care for this poor body of mine according to his providence, whether I suffer much or have some consolation. Why am I anxious? The Lord is near.

St. Martin I

BLESSED KATERI TEKAKWITHA (1656-1680)

BLESSED KATERI TEKAKWITHA was born at Auriesville, New York, in 1656 to a Christian Algonquin and a Mohawk Indian chief. She suffered the loss of her father and mother at the age of four in an epidemic of smallpox which left her disfigured. In 1675, she embraced the Catholic faith through her contacts with Jesuit missionaries, namely Fr. Jacques de Lamberville. Her strong faith caused her to be persecuted among her own people, so she journeyed nearly 200 miles to a Christian Indian village near Montreal, Canada. While there, Kateri dedicated her life to God and lived an exemplary Christian life. She died in 1680 at the age of twenty-four at Caughnawaga, Canada. She is known as the Lily of the Mohawks and her example has inspired the Indian communities of North America.

Father,
you give life to all people
and call those afar off to faith.
Give your gifts to those who do not know you.

ST. ANSELM
(1033-1109) bishop and doctor

ST. ANSELM was born at Aosta, Italy, in 1033. He entered the monastery of Bec in Normandy, France, in 1060 at the age of twenty-seven and was befriended by the great abbot, Lanfranc. He excelled in the study of philosophy and theology and was named prior of the monastery after only a few years. In 1078, he was elected abbot of Bec.

In 1093, Lafranc, Archbishop of Canterbury, England, died and Anselm was elected to succeed him. Upon accepting his post, Anselm began to meet opposition from King William Rutus who tried unsuccessfully to control him. He went to Rome in 1097 to plead his case before Pope Urban I and remained there in exile.

King William Rufus died in 1100 and Anselm returned to his diocese. King Henry I, the new ruler, opposed Anselm concerning the right of investiture and the political and economic power of the Church in England. In 1103, Anselm again went to Rome and met with Pope Paschal II. As before, Anselm found himself supported fully by Rome, but was in exile from 1103 to 1107. Upon his return to England, there was a reconciliation with King Henry and they both came to regard each other with reverence and respect.

Besides learning and administrative ability, Anselm had a warmth and charm that permeated his writings and his relations with others. He strongly opposed slavery and upheld the rights of the Church against the secular power. Anselm died at Canterbury in 1109.

> Lord,
>> while here on earth let me know you better,
>> so that in heaven I may know you completely.
>
> Let my love for you grow deeper here,
> so that I may love you there completely.
>
> Here on earth I shall rejoice in hope,
> in heaven my rejoicing shall be complete
> when my hope is fulfilled.
>
> St. Anselm

ST. GEORGE   April 23
(fourth century) martyr

HISTORICALLY, VERY little is known of St. George's life. According to tradition, he was a Christian soldier who suffered martyrdom about the year 303 in Palestine, sometime before the reign of the Emperor Constantine. A legend beginning in the twelfth century and later popularized in the thirteenth century by a book called *The Golden Legend* tells of George as a Christian soldier born in Cappadocia. In Sylene, Libya, he rescued the king's daughter from a dragon and in turn killed it. As a result, thousands of people were baptized and led to God.

Devotion to George spread to the West during the Crusades when he was invoked for protection by King Richard I of England and his army. St. George is the patron saint of England as well as Portugal, Germany, Aragon, Genoa and Venice.

> Lord,
>> we praise your power that enabled your saints
>> to be strong in life and in face of death.
>> Give us help too in our weakness.

ST. FIDELIS
OF SIGMARINGEN
April 24
(1578-1622) priest and martyr

ST. FIDELIS, whose baptismal name was Mark Rey, was born at Sigmaringen, Germany, in 1578. He attended the University of Freiburg in Breisgau and studied law. About 1610, he received his doctorate in law and became known for his honesty and advocacy of causes for the poor. As a result, he was called "the Poor Man's Lawyer."

Because of his concern for the poor, Fidelis gave up his law practice and entered the Capuchin branch of the Franciscans. His preaching and zeal for the Catholic faith, as well as his care for the needy, prompted the Bishop of Grüsch, Switzerland, to request that he preach among the Protestants of his region. Despite many warnings, Fidelis accepted the invitation.

On April 24, 1622, he addressed a crowd at Grüsch and his persuasive instructions and holiness won a new hearing for Catholicism among the people. Fidelis then went to Seewis to speak before more people. Before he could finish, someone in the crowd tried to shoot and kill him, but they did not succeed. He immediately left Seewis to return to Grüsch. Along the way, he was met by a mob demanding that he deny his faith. When he refused, they beat him to death as he called on God to forgive them. The year was 1622.

Lord, my faith is your gift,
the solid rock on which I stand.
Keep my eyes fixed on the Cross of your Son,
that I may share in his death and resurrection.
St. Fidelis

ST. MARK   April 25
(first century) evangelist

ST. MARK, author of the second Gospel, was a member of the early Christian community at Jerusalem. St. Paul and St. Barnabas, his cousin, took him on their first missionary journey. When they reached Cyprus, however, Mark left them to return to Jerusalem, perhaps because he missed home. This caused

Paul to question for awhile Mark's reliability as a missionary, and the incident brought about a disagreement between himself and Barnabas. Later, Mark became Paul's trusted companion at Rome, during one of Paul's imprisonments. He was also an associate of Peter.

One tradition relates that Mark became Bishop of Alexandria in Egypt. Around the ninth century, his relics were brought to Venice where they rest in the great Cathedral of San Marco.

Mark is depicted in art as a winged lion, probably suggested by the description in his Gospel of John the Baptist as "a voice crying in the desert." It is believed that he wrote his Gospel between 60 and 70 A.D.

> God, our Father,
>> may we know your Son, Jesus Christ,
>> truly one of us and truly God.

ST. PETER CHANEL   April 28
(1803-1841) priest and martyr

ST. PETER CHANEL was born at Cuet, in the diocese of Belley, France, in 1803. He was educated by Abbé Trompier, a parish priest, and eventually entered the seminary. Upon ordination, Peter was assigned to the parish of Crozet. Though the parish was in a less than desirable area and had a bad reputation, he won the hearts of his people by his zeal and kindness to the poor and sick. Peter remained there for three years, but he longed to become a missionary in foreign lands.

In 1831, he joined the Marists and was assigned to the seminary of Belley. In 1836, Peter journeyed to preach the Gospel in the islands of the Pacific, where the name of Christ was unknown. Joining him on the island of Futuna in the New Hebrides were a lay brother and an English layman, Thomas Boog. The inhabitants of Futuna had recently given up cannibalism.

At first, the missionaries met with little success, but gradually their care of the sick and their patience caused a dedicated band of natives to embrace the Catholic faith. However, Niuliki, a local chieftain, was afraid of the Christian influence on his island. This fear was aggravated when Peter converted and baptized his son. Niuliki sent a band of warriors to kill Peter and on April 28, 1841, he was clubbed to death and cut to pieces with swords. After his death, Futuna converted to Catholicism. The flourishing churches of Oceania today honor St. Peter as their founder.

> *Lord of the harvest,*
>   *send laborers to those*
>   *who do not know you, to bring them life.*

ST. CATHERINE OF SIENA   April 29
(1347-1380) virgin

THE YOUNGEST of twenty-five children, St. Catherine was born at Siena, Italy, in 1347 to a wealthy businessman, Giacomo Benincasa and his wife, Lapa. As a young girl of six, while walking home one day, she had a remarkable vision of Jesus. Seated in glory with Sts. Peter, Paul and John, he smiled upon her. From that time on, Catherine wished to give herself to prayer and the service of God.

Her parents, wishing her married with all the advantages they could give her, at first tried to prevent her. Finally they realized that God had favored her and Catherine became a Dominican tertiary at the age of sixteen. She lived at home while following the rule recommended for those seeking God.

She began to nurse the sick in the Siena hospitals, preferring cancer patients and lepers whom others found too difficult to care for. In a vision, Jesus told her, "I desire to come closer to you through the love you have for your neighbor." Gradually, a number of companions were drawn to her to share her inspiration and work. When an epidemic of plague broke out, a friend wrote, "She was always with the plague-stricken. She prepared them for death, she buried them with her own hands. I myself witnessed the joy with which she nursed them and how effective her words were." Frequently, Catherine went to the prisons to counsel those condemned to death and prepare them for their final ordeal.

Her reputation for holiness and wisdom spread not only in Siena, but also in the neighboring cities of Pisa, Lucca, and Florence. Families and rival political parties called on her to mediate their disputes and reconcile their differences.

While on a trip to Pisa in 1375, Catherine received the stigmata. In 1376, she went to Avignon, France to mediate the armed conflict between Florence and the papal government, but her efforts failed. More important, she was able to convince Pope Gregory XI to return to Rome for the good of the Church. When he died, Pope Urban VI was elected in Rome and a rival Pope, Clement VII, was installed in Avignon. This is considered to be the beginning of the "great schism." Catherine went to Rome in 1378 to try and end the dispute, as she was a staunch defender of Pope Urban VI. She died in Rome honored for her sanctity on April 29, 1380, at the age of thirty-three.

Eternal God,
  You are my creator,
  and I am the work of your hands.
  In the blood of your Son you have created me anew;
  Remade by him, I am your beloved.
  Eternal God, limitless and deeper than the sea,
  what more can you give me than yourself?
  An ever-burning fire, you are never consumed.
  In your heat, you burn away my soul's self-love.

You are the fire that takes away all cold.
Your light enables me to know all truth.
Your light is above all light,
  enlightening my mind,
  making the light of faith clear,
  perfecting it so that I may see my own soul alive,
and in this light I receive you—the true light.

St. Catherine of Siena

ST. PIUS V   April 30
(1504-1572) pope

ST. PIUS V, baptized Antonio Michael Ghislieri, was born at Bosco, near Alesssandria, Italy, in 1504. He entered the Dominican Order at the age of fourteen and was ordained in 1528. He taught theology and philosophy in Dominican schools for sixteen years and was chosen Bishop of Nepi and Sutri by Pope Paul IV in 1556. In 1557, he was appointed inquisitor general and cardinal, and in 1559 Bishop of Mondovi.

Pope Pius IV died in December, 1565. Cardinal Ghislieri was elected Pope on January 7, 1566, and adopted the name Pope Pius V. Many of the Church reforms in worship and ministry sought by the Council of Trent were carried out by Pope Pius V. His holy life and care for the poor created a new atmosphere in Rome. He was responsible for the publication of a new catechism, missal and breviary. In 1570, he excommunicated Queen Elizabeth I of England.

Pius dedicated himself to healing the wounds caused by the Reformation. His support of Don Juan of Austria succeeded in preventing a Turkish invasion of Europe. When Don Juan and Marcantonio Colonna defeated the Turks at the Battle of Lepanto on October 7, 1571, Pius instituted the Feast of the Holy Rosary in thanksgiving to the Blessed Virgin for her support of the Christian cause. He died on May 1, 1572.

Lord, give us dedication to truth
and strength to stand firm for what is right.

MAY

ST. JOSEPH THE WORKER   May 1

ON MAY 1, 1955, Pope Puis XII addressed the Catholic Association of Italian Workers and declared that this day would be known as the feast day of St. Joseph the Worker. In the Communist bloc, May 1 is celebrated as May Day, which glorifies the relationship between the worker and the socialist state. It is obvious that the Church was very concerned with this, and wanted to demonstrate to its faithful that it was equally concerned about the plight of the working man and woman.

Joseph, a carpenter, taught his trade to his son, Jesus, and provided for his family. It is especially important to remember this human element when contemplating the lives of both St. Joseph and the Holy Family.

> Lord God, *maker of all things,*
> *you give us skill of mind and body*
> *to labor and serve in this world.*
>
> *May we follow the way of St. Joseph*
> *who worked with Christ at his side,*
> *and may all we do be a sign of*
> *your greatness and power.*

ST. ATHANASIUS
(295-373) bishop and doctor

ST. ATHANASIUS was born at Alexandria, in 295. His parents were Christians and he received an excellent education. His faith was influenced by Christians who were persecuted at the hands of Roman authorities. From them he learned to defend the truth God revealed with courage and constancy.

In 318, he became a deacon and became secretary to Bishop Alexander of Alexandria. In 323, the priest Arius began to teach that Jesus Christ was not God, but only a good man. The Council of Nicaea, which Athanasius attended in 325, condemned Arianism as untrue and adopted the Nicene Creed as a confession of faith for all Catholics. Until his death nearly fifty years later, he would refute Arianism with forceful logic, using the words of Scripture to proclaim the Church's true belief. Jesus was truly divine, God's only Son, the same nature as the Father and the Holy Spirit.

Bishop Alexander died and Athanasius succeeded him as Bishop of Alexandria in 327. Many supporters of Arius, especially Eusebius, the Arian Bishop of Nicomedia, were influential at the court of Emperor Constantine and tried to discredit Athanasius. He attended the Council of Tyre in 335 and was exiled to Trier, Germany, by Emperor Constantine in 336. In all, Athanasius was exiled five times for a total of seventeen years while he was Bishop of Alexandria. He was recalled to Alexan-

dria for the last time in 365 by Emperor Valens and remained there until his death on May 2, 373.

Athanasius upheld the Christian faith before all odds. Even in fierce controversy, he reached out tolerantly to those who were led astray. St. Gregory Nazianzen called him "the pillar of the Church," and because of his staunch defense of Christian beliefs, he is counted among the great teachers of early Christianity. Athanasius is also considered to be one of the great Doctors of the Church.

Father, your Word was made flesh.
May we welcome your Son among us.

ST. PHILIP   (first century)   May 3
and
ST. JAMES   (d. 62) apostles

ST. PHILIP was born at Bethsaida in Galilee. He was one of the apostles and a disciple of John the Baptist. Philip heard the call of Jesus, "Follow me," and accompanied Jesus on his public ministry. He is mentioned in St. John's Gospel, and invited the apostle, Bartholomew, to come and see Christ. At the Last Supper he said to Jesus, "Lord, show us the Father, and it is enough."

According to tradition, Philip was present with the apostles who spent ten days waiting in the upper room in Jerusalem for the coming of the Holy

Spirit at Pentecost. After the death of Christ, Philip preached the Gospel in Phrygia, Asia Minor. He was martyred at Hierapolis by soldiers loyal to Emperor Domitian.

St. James, also known as James the Less, was one of the twelve apostles and is called "the son of Alpheus" and "the brother of the Lord" in the Gospels. It is assumed, however, that he was most likely a cousin of Jesus. He is believed to be the author of the Epistle of St. James in the New Testament.

James was appointed the Bishop of Jerusalem and was present at the Council of Jerusalem. He was also present with the apostles in the upper room awaiting the coming of the Holy Spirit at Pentecost. James remained in Jerusalem after Pentecost and was stoned to death there in 62.

O God, give us faith through the
words of your apostles.

ST. NEREUS   (first century)   May 12
and
ST. ACHILLEUS   (first century)   martyrs

ACCORDING TO early Roman tradition, Sts. Nereus and Achilleus were soldiers of the Roman army who gave up their commissions when they embraced the Christian faith. Because of this, they were exiled to the island of Terracina and then beheaded. They were buried in the cemetery of Domitilla. An ancient church built by Pope Siricius in 390 still stands over their burial site in Rome on the Ardeatine Way.

> *Lord, wipe away the tears of those*
> *who suffer for your name.*
> *Give courage to all who*
> *are persecuted for their faith.*

ST. PANCRAS
(d. 304) martyr

May 12

ST. PANCRAS, according to early Roman tradition, was born at Phrygia and was orphaned. He was brought to Rome by an uncle and became a Christian. As a young boy of fourteen, he was beheaded for his beliefs during the reign of Diocletian about 304. He was buried in the cemetery of Calepodius, on the Aurelian Way, and a church was built to mark his grave by Pope Symmachus. Some of his relics were carried to England. St. Pancras Church in London is named after him and a church in Canterbury was dedicated in his honor.

> *Lord, you were with the three young men*
> *in the fiery furnace,*
> *and blessed St. Pancras with courage*
> *to confess your name.*
> *Be with our young people*
> *and make their faith strong.*

ST. MATTHIAS
(first century) apostle

May 14

ACCORDING TO the Acts of the Apostles, St. Matthias was chosen to replace Judas Iscariot as one of the twelve apostles after the resurrection of Jesus. Two men, Barsabbas and Matthias, were proposed, but only one was selected. A companion of Christ during his public ministry, Matthias was among the seventy-two disciples whom Jesus sent out to preach. He was also a witness to Christ's resurrection.

Tradition says that he preached the Gospel in Judea, Cappadocia, and near the Caspian Sea. He suffered martyrdom by crucifixion at Colchis.

> *Lord God,*
> *make us disciples of your Son,*
> *hearers and doers of his word,*
> *witnesses for him in this world.*

ST. ISIDORE THE FARMER
(1070-1130)

May 15

ST. ISIDORE was born at Madrid, Spain, in 1070 to a poor family. At an early age, he was employed by John de Vergas, a wealthy landowner, as a farm laborer to work on his estate outside Madrid. His wife, Maria Torribia, is also venerated as a saint known as St. Maria de la Cabeza. After the birth of their son, who died at a young age, they dedicated their lives to God.

Besides his work, Isidore was devoted to prayer and to the Church. He would wake up early every day and go to church. After Mass he would commune with God, the saints, and his guardian angel, as he worked with his plow in the fields. Though a poor man, he found it possible to share much of his own resources with the needy. According to those who knew him, he worked miracles to feed the hungry. He also loved animals and provided grain for them in winter and times of drought. His simple life was filled with a sense of God, and after his death on May 15, 1130, many miracles were attributed to his intercession. He is the patron of farmers.

Lord, bless our work and
make fruitful the things we do.

ST. JOHN I   May 18
(d. 526) pope and martyr

ST. JOHN was born at Tuscany, Italy and was elected Pope in 523 upon the death of Pope Hormisidas. King Theodoric the Goth ruled Italy at that time, and he fully supported Arianism. Because of his beliefs, he was in conflict with the Byzantine Emperor, Justin, who was a staunch defender of the Catholic faith.

In 523, Justin issued a decree demanding all Arians in his empire to relinquish their churches to the Catholic Church. King Theodoric was greatly angered and sent John to Constantinople to mediate the dispute. Theodoric was also very suspicious of the increasing friendship between the Eastern and Western Churches, for he saw it as a threat to his own rule.

When Pope John I returned to Rome, he found out that Theodoric had murdered his father-in-law, Symmachus, and the great philosopher, Boethius. King Theodoric heard of the burgeoning friendship between John and Emperor Justin and was convinced that a conspiracy was being planned against him. He had John imprisoned at Ravenna, where he died about 526 from the cruel conditions he experienced.

> *Lord, you open your arms to all*
> *who suffer persecution unjustly.*
> *Have mercy on those*
> *who cry out for justice.*

ST. BERNARDINE OF SIENA May 20
(1380-1444) priest

ST. BERNARDINE OF SIENA was born in Massa Marittima, Italy, in 1380 to a noble and wealthy family—his father was the governor of the town. Orphaned at the age of seven, Bernardine was raised by his aunt and her daughter. At the age of eleven, he was sent to be educated in Siena, and his intelligence and good disposition won him many friends.

He joined the Confraternity of our Lady at the age of seventeen. In 1400, a plague struck Siena and Bernardine volunteered to help manage the hospital of Santa Maria della Scala. With the help of companions, he made sure that the sick were taken care of. Several of his companions died, and Bernardine was overcome by fever.

In 1403, he entered the Franciscans and was ordained. He spent the next several years in solitude and reflection at the convent of Colombaio outside Siena. In 1417, he began to preach with increasing success throughout all of Italy. The crowds were so great that he often preached in village squares instead of churches.

Pope Martin V offered him the bishopric of Siena in 1427, but Bernardine declined. He would later decline the bishoprics of Ferrara and Urbino. In 1430, he became vicar general of the Friars of the Strict Observance. In 1442, he resigned this office in order to continue his missionary work.

Bernardine was devoted to the Holy Name of Jesus and inspired those to whom he spoke with a similar love. The Italy of his time was divided into many political factions, with each proclaiming its particular affiliation in signs and banners. Bernardine made people recall their common faith in

Christ, which was more important than any other allegiance. Worn out from his labors, he died in Aquila on his way to preach in Naples on May 20, 1444.

> *Lord, we sing and bless your name.*
> *Before all peoples and at all times*
> *we remember you, for we bear the*
> *name of your Son, Jesus Christ.*

VENERABLE BEDE   May 25
(673-735) priest and doctor

ST. BEDE was born at Wearmouth-Jarrow, England, in 673. As a young boy, he entered St. Peter and St. Paul Monastery in Wearmouth-Jarrow and was educated by the Benedictine abbots. He found great joy in learning and also in living the monastic life. Bede spent all of his life in the monastery, except for a few visits to local places.

While in the monastery, he became a monk. He was ordained in 703 at the age of thirty. Bede was and still is acknowledged as one of the great scholars of his time. His commentaries on the Holy Scriptures and writings of the early saints were avidly sought by his contemporaries for their wisdom and warm spirituality. In 731, he completed his masterpiece, *Ecclesiastical History*, which is the primary source of the history of England, the

English Church and Christianity in England up until 729.

The title, "Venerable," was an affectionate tribute from his fellow religious. The monastery at Wearmouth-Jarrow became a beacon from which his light would shine upon the whole world. Bede died as he lived, in 735, working tirelessly on a commentary on the Gospel of John.

I pray, loving Jesus, that as you graciously allowed me to drink with delight your words of knowledge, so you would mercifully grant me to come one day to you, the fountain of all wisdom, and appear before you face to face.

Venerable Bede

ST. GREGORY VII   May 25
(1028-1085) pope

ST. GREGORY VII was born in Tuscany, Italy, in 1028 and baptized Hildebrand. He was educated at a monastery in Rome and became a monk at Cluny in 1047. He served faithfully in the administration of the Church as secretary to Pope Gregory VI and counselor to Pope Leo IX. Pope Alexander II died in 1073 and Hildebrand was elected to succeed him.

As Pope Gregory VII, he sought the reforms of the Church which had begun with Pope Leo IX. At that time, the Church suffered from simony, lay investiture, and marriage of the clergy. Many secular rulers controlled the appointment of bishops and other Church officials within their lands. Often their appointments were unqualified or unworthy, with the result that the Church's relgous life was seriously harmed.

Gregory's demand that the Church alone should appoint its bishops brought him into conflict with the kings and rulers of Europe, especially Emperor Henry IV of Germany, all of whom were in favor of lay investiture. Because of his beliefs, Henry was excommunicated by Pope Gregory. In 1077, fearing for his political future because of being excommunicated, Henry went to Conossa, Italy, to beg Gregory's pardon, which was granted.

However, the struggle for the power of appointment continued through Pope Gregory's reign. Henry invaded Italy in 1084 and vanquished Rome. He installed an anti-pope, Clement III, and banished Pope Gregory. Gregory was saved by Robert Guiscard, Duke of Normandy, but still had to leave Rome. He died in exile in Salerno on May 25, 1085. His last words were, "I have loved right and hated evil, so I die in exile."

Lord, make us fearless workers for truth whatever the cost.

ST. MARY MAGDALENE DE PAZZI   (1566-1607) virgin

ST. MARY MAGDALENE DE PAZZI was born in Florence, Italy, in 1566 to a distinguished and noble family. As a young girl, she was drawn to the religious life. She entered the Carmelite convent in Florence at the age of seventeen and led a life of prayer and holiness for twenty-five years. In her many personal trials and illnesses she looked to the Cross of Christ, from which she drew comfort and patience, and experienced deep spiritual consolation. She dictated a number of writings, the most famous being *Admonisitions*, and believed her vocation was to pray for reform in the Church and for the conversion of mankind. A wise teacher and guide for her sister companions, she was revered during life and honored after her death in 1607.

> *Come Holy Spirit,*
>   *precious pearl of the Father*
>   *and delight of the Word.*
> *Come, reward of the saints,*
>   *comforter of souls,*
>   *light in darkness,*
>   *wealth of the poor,*
>   *food of the hungry,*
>   *all treasures are found in you.*
>
> St. Mary Magdalene de Pazzi

ST. PHILIP NERI
(1515-1595) priest

BORN IN Florence, Italy, in 1515, St. Philip Neri was known as a child for his good disposition and cheerfulness. He enjoyed a good family life and the company of religious people.

As a young man of eighteen, he went to the town of San Germano near Rome to work for a wealthy cousin who wished him to inherit his business in time. In a short while, however, Philip was overwhelmed with a desire to follow Jesus' counsel, "Blessed are the poor in spirit." In 1533, he left his cousin's house and went to Rome to live as a poor man dependent upon what God would send him.

For three years, he studied philosophy and theology at the Sapienza and at Sant'Agostino. Then selling his books and giving what money he had to the poor, he began a life of prayer and service to the sick and the poor. His warm personality and lively faith attracted many people from all levels of Roman society to seek his confidence. He arranged for groups of people to meet frequently for prayer, study, conversation, and the enjoyment of music and sport. At the same time, he encouraged them to visit the sick and care for the many pilgrims who visited Rome. In 1548, with the help of Fr. Persiano Rossa, Philip founded the Confraternity of the Most Holy Trinity, an organization of lay people dedicated to the care of sick and needy pilgrims.

Philip loved the old churches and shrines of

Rome where so many early saints are honored. He loved especially the catacombs, where the early Christians are buried surrounded by reminders of their strong faith in Christ. Philip led regular pilgrimages to these holy places and brought those who accompanied him to a new appreciation of their faith.

At a time when the Roman Church was weakened by laxity in its clergy and government, and the Protestant Reformation threatened to destroy the Catholic Church, Philip encouraged many Christians in Rome to personal holiness. Great saints like Ignatius Loyola, Charles Borromeo, and Pius V looked on him as a friend. He is one of the great figures in the Counter Reformation of the Catholic Church.

On May 23, 1551, he was ordained a priest. Later that year, Philip formed the Congregation of the Oratory, whose members would encourage people to deepen their faith. This organization received formal approval from Pope Gregory XIII in 1575. A biographer says of Philip that "one ideal of his life was to do much without appearing to do anything." He desired deeply the reform of the Catholic Church and chose to work for it not through severity but through gentleness, cheerfulness, and friendship. He died in Rome on May 26, 1595, at eighty years of age.

Father, you love a cheerful giver;
may I give what I have with joy.

ST. AUGUSTINE   May 27
OF CANTERBURY   (d. 605) bishop

ST. AUGUSTINE OF CANTERBURY, was prior of the monastery of St. Andrew in Rome. In 596, at the request of Pope Gregory the Great, he led a party of about thirty of his monks to England to preach the Gospel. Warned about possible dangers from crossing the channel and from the Anglo-Saxons, the band hesitated on the shores of France. After receiving further encouragement from the Pope, however, they made the crossing and entered the territory of King Ethelbert of Kent, who permitted them to preach to his people. By the next year, the king and many of his people were baptized.

Soon after, Augustine went to France, but eventually, he was appointed Bishop of England. He built a church and monastery at Canterbury and helped to establish dioceses in London and Rochester.

Augustine sought to spread the faith throughout England and to reconcile older groups of Christians who had been driven into the remote corners of the country by Anglo-Saxon warriors.

He died on May 26, 605.

> *Lord, grant that your word be preached*
> *to all the world,*
> *and lead all peoples to your kingdom.*

THE VISITATION OF MARY   May 31

CELEBRATED BETWEEN the feasts of the Annunciation (March 25) and the Birth of John the Baptist (June 24), the feast of the Visitation originated in the Church of the Middle Ages. It recalls Mary's visit to her cousin, Elizabeth, after the angel announced that she was to be the mother of Jesus. Filled with the Holy Spirit, these two great women recognized the power of God at work in their midst. "Blessed are you among women," Elizabeth said, "and blessed is the fruit of your womb."

Mary replied:

My soul proclaims the greatness of the Lord,
my spirit rejoices in God my Savior
for he has looked with favor on his lowly servant.

From this day all generations will call me blessed:
the Almighty has done great things for me,
and holy is his Name.

He has mercy on those who fear him
in every generation.

He has shown the strength of his arm,
he has scattered the proud in their conceit.

He has cast down the mighty from their thrones,
and has lifted up the lowly.

He has filled the hungry with good things,
and the rich he has sent away empty.

He has come to the help of his servant Israel
for he has remembered his promise of mercy,
the promise he made to our fathers,
to Abraham and his children forever.

JUNE

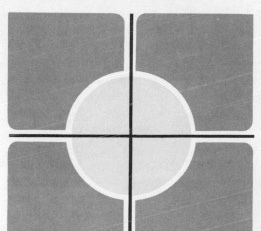

ST. JUSTIN   June 1
   (100-165) martyr

ST. JUSTIN was born at Nablus, Palestine, about the year 100 to a family of pagan Greek origin. As a young man he looked for truth from the many philosophies and teachers of his time, especially Plato. However, he found Platonism wanting and lacking the answers to his questions. Walking along the seashore one day, he met an old man who asked him what he was looking for. Justin answered, "The meaning of life." The stranger replied that only God could teach him that, and told him to turn to the Christian faith that Jesus Christ revealed. After prayer and study, Justin became a Christian when he was about thirty years old.

From his own experience, Justin knew there were many people like himself searching for truth, so he began writing and teaching about Christianity in Rome and other great cities. He addressed himself to Emperor Antoninus, the Roman Senate, and the influential teachers and figures of his time. Not only did he propose the beauty and wisdom of his faith, but he also answered those who misrepresented or ridiculed the Christian religion.

He is considered to be the first Christian 'apologist,' or defender of the faith, of the second century. His two great writings are *Apologies* and *Dialogue with Trypho*.

Justin opened a school in Rome where his teaching increasingly disturbed the authorities. At the in-

116

stigation of the Cynic philosopher, Crescens, whom he defeated in a debate, Justin was denounced as a Christian and arrested with six companions. The Roman court records contain this account of his trial:

Rusticus, the Roman Prefect: "Listen, you are supposed to be an eloquent man and believe you have the truth. If you are beheaded, do you think you will go to heaven?"

Justin: "I hope to be rewarded for keeping Christ's teachings, if I suffer as you say."

Rusticus: "Come here and sacrifice to the gods."

Justin: "No one in his right mind does anything false, when he knows what is true."

Rusticus: "You will be tortured without mercy, if you don't do what I tell you."

Justin: "Nothing is better than to suffer for Jesus Christ and so to be saved. Then we can stand confidently before the judgment seat of God, when all this world passes away."

Justin and the six other Christians who were on trial were sentenced to be scourged and then beheaded for their faith in Jesus Christ. He died in 165.

May we also reject falsehood and remain loyal to our Lord Jesus Christ.

ST. MARCELLINUS
and
ST. PETER (d. 304) martyrs

ACCORDING TO tradition Sts. Marcellinus and Peter were Christians martyred in Rome during the persecution of Diocletian about the year 304. Marcellinus was a priest and Peter was an exorcist. Their bodies were hidden after their execution and buried on the Via Labicana, but were subsequently discovered and honored in the city of Rome. Pope Damasus, who composed an inscription over their tomb, related that as a boy he heard the details of their execution from the executioner himself. They are named in the Roman Canon (Eucharistic Prayer I) of the Mass.

Father, give us faith and hope to endure
with patience the trials that come to us.

ST. CHARLES LWANGA
and COMPANIONS (d. 1886) martyrs

THE MARTYRDOM of St. Charles Lwanga and his twenty-one companions in Uganda, Africa, during the years 1885-1886, was a decisive factor in the remarkable spread of Christianity on that continent in this century. Cardinal Lavigerie's White Fathers were Catholic missionaries who reached that

remote part of the world in 1879 and succeeded in converting a number of native Africans, some of whom were servants of King Mwanga, a local Ugandan ruler. However, by 1885, King Mwanga began to persecute Christians.

Charles Lwanga was the master of pages in the court of King Mwanga. The king wished to enlist some of the pages in his court for immoral purposes. When the Christian pages refused, he began to threaten them with torture and death. They followed the example set by Charles, their leader, and steadfastly refused King Mwanga's advances. Summoning them before him, the king asked if they intended to remain Christian. "Till death!" they responded. "Then put them to death!" the ruler angrily shouted.

On the road to their execution in Namugongo, three pages died. However, many bystanders were amazed at the courage and calm of Charles Lwanga and his companions. On Ascension Day, June 3, 1886, they were each wrapped in a mat of reeds and set afire for their faith. In the following year, the number of converts to Christianity multiplied at an extraordinary rate. The prayer for their feast praises their example:

> *Father,*
> *you have made the blood of martyrs*
> *the seed of Christians.*

ST. BONIFACE

(673-754) bishop and martyr

ST. BONIFACE is called the Apostle of Germany because the spread of Christianity among the German tribes of central Europe was due largely to his efforts. Baptized Winfrid, Boniface was born at Crediton in Devonshire, England, in 673. He decided to become a monk after listening to the conversation of some monastic visitors to his home when he was a child. At the age of seven, he entered a monastery near Exeter; at fourteen, he entered the Benedictine Abbey of Nursling. He was tutored by the abbot, Winbert, and became director of the abbey. Boniface became a skilled teacher of languages and Scripture and was ordained in 715.

Yet he longed to go as a missionary to the German people, among whom some English monks were already laboring. In 718, in Rome, he presented himself to Pope Gregory II, who commissioned him to preach the Gospel of Christ in Germany. The rulers of that land received him favorably and his skill in language enabled him to speak the word of God to them and their people in ways they could understand.

Boniface tried to eradicate pagan superstition which hindered Christian belief. One day, he went to Mt. Gudenberg at Geismar with an axe in hand to a sacred oak tree, venerated by the pagans for its magic powers. The huge tree crashed to the ground before his blows, while a great crowd watched in disbelief that their pagan gods could not withstand this lone Christian missionary. Happy with his success, Boniface left for Thuringia to continue his ministry.

In 722, Pope Gregory II appointed Boniface as bishop over all of Germany and gave him permission to set up dioceses and bishoprics where he saw fit. Inspired by his zeal, other English monks and nuns came to Germany to teach Christianity and establish monasteries in Ohrdruf, Reichenau, Murbach, Fritzlar and Fulda, as centers of faith and civilization. In 747, Boniface established his see at Mainz and was appointed primate of Germany by Pope Zachary. He was also chosen apostolic delegate for Germany and Gaul by Pope Zachary.

Not only Germany, but also France was influenced by Boniface's concern for the Church. Through his efforts, the German Church was reorganized and both dioceses and monasteries were reformed and renewed in spirit. He also successfully recalled the Frankish rulers to their Christian mission.

On June 5, 754, the eve of Pentecost, Boniface was preparing to confirm a large group of newly baptized converts at Dokkum, Holland. While he was in a tent preparing for the ceremony, a band of pagans burst in and killed him. The group of converts was also murdered. Boniface is buried at Fulda. He died faithful to the Church he loved. As he wrote himself, "In her voyage across the ocean of this world, the Church is like a ship pounded by

the waves of life's different stresses. Our duty is not
to abandon ship, but to keep her on course."

Lord,
  Your martyr Boniface spread the faith by his
  teaching and died for his beliefs.

ST. NORBERT   June 6
   (1080-1134) bishop

ST. NORBERT was born at Xanten, in the duchy of
Cleves, Prussia, in 1080. His was a noble family and
at first, he led a carefree life as a cleric and court official under Emperor Henry V.

One day, Norbert was riding his horse near Wreden
and was caught in a thunderstorm. He was thrown
from his horse and, much like St. Paul on the road
to Damascus, heard a voice calling him to the holy
life. He immediately changed his way of living and
was ordained in 1115. He was denounced by the
Council of Fritzlar in 1118 and gave away all his
wealth to the poor. He then went to Languedoc
where Pope Gelasius II gave him permission to
preach the word of Christ wherever he felt it was
necessary.

Norbert began to preach in France and was joined
by Blessed Hugh of Fosses, a devoted companion.
In 1121, at Prémontré, with forty companions, he
founded the Order of Premonstratensians. In time,

he would establish a number of monasteries and convents. He was appointed Bishop of Magdeburg in 1126 by Emperor Lothair II.

Norbert inspired a reform of Church life and directed new missionary efforts among non-Christians. He was a staunch defender of the papacy and became a good friend of St. Bernard. An eloquent preacher and spokesman for the Church, Norbert died on June 6, 1134, in Magdeburg.

> *Father, give your Church*
> *true shepherds to guide your people.*

ST. EPHREM   June 9
(306-373) deacon and doctor

ST. EPHREM was born at Nisibis, Mesopotamia in 306. He was baptized at the age of eighteen and became a companion of the Bishop of Nisibis, St. James. It is thought that he might have accompanied James to the Council of Nicaea in 325. Nisibis was handed over to the Persians by Emperor Jovian in 363. Ephrem left immediately and retreated to a cave in the mountains overlooking Edessa. A poet and hymn writer, he wrote many hymns while in Edessa. He gave the Church of his day many compositions for its liturgy and devotion. He was known as "the Harp of the Holy Spirit." Ephrem was revered by other great saints, such as St.

Jerome, for his deep faith and wisdom. In 370, he went to Caesarea to visit St. Basil, and in 372, Ephrem organized an extensive program for victims of famine in his native land. Weakened by his many labors, he died at Edessa in 373. He is a Doctor of the Church.

Lord, shine on our darkened souls
  your great light of wisdom
  that we may see and so serve you.
Only in sunlight can we go about our tasks;
  give us day without end so that we may know
  your risen life.

St. Ephrem

ST. BARNABAS   June 11
  (first century) apostle

THOUGH NOT one of the twelve apostles chosen by Jesus, St. Barnabas played an important role in the mission of the apostles to the Gentile world. He was a Jew of the tribe of Levi and was born at Cyprus. His name was Joseph, but was changed to Barnabas by the apostles. He was one of the first converts to Christianity at Jerusalem after Pentecost. The Acts of the Apostles describes him as Barnabas, "the Son of Encouragement," who "sold a field which belonged to him and brought the money and laid it at the apostles' feet."

"A good man, filled with the Holy Spirit and with faith," he was closely connected with St. Paul during his early missionary journeys and introduced him to the apostles. As a founder of the Church at Antioch, Barnabas invited Paul from Tarsus to help him form the new community of Christians. Then, inspired by the Holy Spirit, Paul and Barnabas journeyed to other cities of Asia Minor, preaching the message of Jesus Christ.

The two apostles brought money from the Church of Antioch for the relief of famine victims in Judea. Barnabas and Paul also spoke at the Council of Jerusalem, describing the success of the Gospel among the Gentiles and winning approval for further journeys to the Gentile world.

The two apostles came to disagreement in the course of their ministry over Barnabas' cousin, John Mark, and separated. Barnabas and John Mark went to Cyprus, and Paul went to Syria. Eventually, they were reunited. There is nothing we know for certain of Barnabas' later activity and death, but it is thought that he was stoned to death in 61 at Salamis.

Father,
> *you sent St. Barnabas to convert the nations.*
> *Help us to proclaim your Gospel.*

ST. ANTHONY OF PADUA   June 13
(1195-1231) priest and doctor

ST. ANTHONY OF PADUA was born at Lisbon, Portugal, in 1195. His surname comes from the Italian city where he lived the latter part of his life. His parents were members of the Portuguese nobility; his father was a knight at the court of King Alfonso II.

His early education took place at the cathedral of Lisbon. At the age of fifteen, he joined the Regular Canons of St. Augustine and was transferred to the monastery at Coîmbra two years later because of distractions caused by his friends' visits. At the monastery, Anthony devoted himself to prayer and study and became a learned scholar of the Bible.

In 1220, Don Pedro of Portugal brought the relics of Franciscans who had been martyred to Coîmbra. This had a tremendous effect on Anthony, who requested admission to the Franciscans. In 1221, he was accepted. Soon after, he set out for Morocco to preach the Gospel to the Moors. On the way to Morocco, he was forced to return to Europe because of illness. On his return home, a storm drove his ship to the shores of Italy, where he would live for the rest of his life.

Upon his return, Anthony went to Assisi, where the general chapter meeting of 1221 took place. At the meeting, he was assigned to the hermitage of San Paolo near Forli. It was in Forli that he gave a great sermon which propelled him into his calling as a preacher.

A gifted preacher, Anthony was also called upon to teach theology to his fellow Franciscans. He was the first member of the Franciscans to be so honored. Anthony drew large crowds wherever he went in Italy, but his greatest success was in Padua where the entire city flocked to hear his word and welcomed him as another St. Francis.

After the death of Francis, Anthony became the minister provincial of Emilia or Romagna. In 1226, he was elected as the envoy from the general chapter to Pope Gregory IX. Soon after, he was released from this duty so he could continue his preaching. He returned to Padua, where he preached until his death. Anthony died on June 13, 1231, at the age of thirty-six. He is a Doctor of the Church.

Lord, may we seek you and then find you.

ST. ROMUALD   June 19
(950-1027) abbot

ST. ROMUALD was born at Ravenna, Italy, in 950 to a noble family. At the age of twenty, he gave up his indulgent style of life to give himself to God alone. Apparently, his father had killed a relative in a duel over property. He entered the San Apollinare Monastery at Classe and became a monk in order to make up for his father's sins.

Three years later, Romuald left San Apollinare

in search of a more disciplined life and became a hermit. Approximately ten years later, Emperor Otto III appointed him abbot of San Apollinare Monastery. Romuald's father, Sergius, had also become a monk, and Romuald was instrumental in guiding his father in the spiritual life. It was also at this time, about 990, that he went to Hungary to convert the Magyars, but was forced to return because of illness.

Romuald grew in wisdom and spiritual insight. His life of solitude and prayer attracted many followers. He spent the rest of his life traveling throughout Italy founding monasteries and hermitages. His most famous monasteries were founded at Vallombrosa in 1012 and Camaldoli in 1023. He also founded the Camaldolese Order. Romuald died at Valdi Castro on June 19, 1027.

> Lord, you are always with us,
>   no need of ours is forgotten.
>   Keep our minds and hearts attentive
>   to your presence.

ST. ALOYSIUS GONZAGA   June 21
(1568-1591) religious

ST. ALOYSIUS GONZAGA was born in the castle of Castiglione delle Stivieri in Lombardy, Italy, on March 9, 1568. His father, Ferrante, was the Marquis of Castiglione and held a high position in the court of King Philip II of Spain. He wanted Aloysius to be a great soldier, but Aloysius had other desires: he wanted to serve God with his body and soul.

In 1577, Aloysius and his brother, Ridolfo, went to Florence to learn Latin and Italian. In 1579, they were placed in the court of the Duke of Mantua, and their father was appointed governor of Montserrat. At the age of twelve, Aloysius was afflicted with a kidney disease which would bother him for the rest of his life.

About this time, Aloysius read a book about Jesuit missionaries in India and became greatly intrigued with the idea of joining the Society of Jesus. He began to live as a monk in the winters at Casale-Monferrato and taught catechism to the poor boys of Castiglione in the summer. In 1581, his father was called to accompany Empress Mary of Austria on her trip from Bohemia to Spain. The family moved to Spain, and Aloysius and his brother were made pages in the court of Prince Don Diego.

Still true to his calling, Aloysius desired to become a Jesuit, but his family would not hear of it. In time, his father capitulated to his desires and Aloysius entered the Jesuit novitiate in Rome in 1585. He went to Milan to study, became a novice, and made his vows in 1587. In 1591, an epidemic broke out in Rome. The Jesuits opened a hospital of their own and Aloysius worked there to help victims of the plague. Aloysius caught the plague, and when told that he had contracted it, he cried out, "I rejoiced when I heard them say: we will go to God's house." To his mother he wrote: "Our parting will not be for long; we shall see each other again in heaven; we shall be united with our Savior..." After receiving viaticum and the last rites from his confessor, St. Robert Bellarmine, Aloysius died on June 21, 1591.

May we who have not followed your innocence follow your example of penance.

ST. PAULINUS OF NOLA   June 22
(355-431) bishop

ST. PAULINUS was born at Bordeaux, France, in 355 to a rich and powerful Roman family. His father was the Roman prefect of Gaul and had extensive land holdings in Gaul and Italy. He was educated in rhetoric and poetry by the poet Ausonius. He also studied law, received his doctorate, and was welcomed into the intellectual and cultural circles of his day.

He married Therasia, a Christian woman from a noble family in Spain and was baptized by Bishop Delphinus of Bordeaux. In 390, he and his wife moved to her estate in Spain. After the death of their only child, they decided to give their lives to God and began to distribute their property and wealth to both the Church and the poor. On Christmas Day in 393, while participating in the liturgy, the people cried out for Paulinus to be a priest. In response, he was ordained by the Bishop of Barcelona.

In 395, Paulinus moved to Nova, Italy, where he had extensive land holdings. As in Spain, he gave away his material possessions to the poor. He ministered at the shrine of St. Felix, an early Christian martyr, and became Bishop of Nola in 409. Paulinus won great respect for his writings and poetry, his hospitality and care of the poor, and his holy way of life. He died in 431.

> *Father, your gift of the Spirit*
> *makes your people one in mind and heart.*
> *Bring us together so that we might serve you*
> *through kindness to our neighbor.*

ST. JOHN FISCHER June 22
(1469-1535) bishop and martyr

ST. JOHN FISCHER was born at Beverley, Yorkshire, England, in 1469. He entered Cambridge University as a student at the age of fourteen. He was ordained at the age of twenty-two and held various positions while at Cambridge: senior proctor, doctor of divinity, and master of Michaelhouse. In 1501, he was elected vice-chancellor of Cambridge, but resigned his post in 1502 to become the chaplain of the king's mother, Lady Margaret Beaufort. He was elected chancellor of Cambridge in 1504, and through his efforts Cambridge grew in prestige as a center of learning. He was also elected Bishop of Rochester in 1504. His learning, holiness, and devotion to his pastoral duties caused the young King Henry VIII to say there was no better bishop anywhere in the world.

King Henry VIII wanted to divorce his wife, Catherine of Aragon, but John Fischer forcefully upheld the validity of their union. Henry was furious at his opposition and when John refused to sign the Oath of Supremacy stating that Henry VIII was head of the English Church, he was arrested and imprisoned. "Not that I condemn anyone else's conscience. Their conscience may save them, and mine must save me." The year was 1534.

While in prison, Pope Paul III made John a cardinal. After ten months in prison, he was sentenced to death. Carrying a small copy of the New Testament, he went to the place of execution. To the crowd gathered there he stated that he was dying for his faith in the Catholic Church and asked their prayers. Then he recited the *Te Deum* and the psalm, "In you I have hoped, O Lord," and was beheaded on June 22, 1535.

Father,
   you confirm true faith with martyrdom.

ST. THOMAS MORE June 22
(1478-1535) martyr

ST. THOMAS MORE was born in London, England, in 1478. He went to Oxford, studied law, and received his doctorate in 1501. He entered the English Parliament in 1504. He married Jane Holt in 1505 and had four children: Margaret, Elizabeth, Cecilia, and John.

The More household was a model of spiritual and intellectual life. Thomas saw that his daughters were well educated—something unusual in those days—and led his family in prayer, reading the Scriptures, and discussion on the important matters of his day. He welcomed into his home not only famous scholars like St. John Fischer and Erasmus, but also his poorer neighbors, whom he treated warmly and respectfully. When Jane died, Thomas married Alice Middleton, a widow, in 1511.

When Henry VIII became king, he sought out More as a friend and advisor. In 1529, Thomas became Lord Chancellor of England and functioned wisely and justly in that office. His friend, Erasmus, wrote: "In serious matters no man is more prized, while if the king wishes to relax no one's conversation is more cheerful...Happy the nation where kings appoint such officials."

Shortly after Thomas took office, Henry VIII began proceedings to divorce Catherine of Aragon. Because he could not agree with the king, Thomas kept silent and eventually, in 1532, he resigned his office.

Without income and in disfavor, he spent the next few years writing and reflecting, living quietly with his family, "being merry together," as he said. But in 1534, he was asked, with John Fischer, to take an oath to the king that he could not accept. He refused and, after fifteen months in prison, he was beheaded on July 6, 1535, "the king's good servant but God's first." He is the patron of lawyers.

In prison he wrote to his daughter, "I trust only in God's merciful goodness. His grace has strengthened me till now and made me content to lose goods, land, and life as well, rather than swear against my conscience. I will not mistrust him, Meg, though I shall feel myself weakening and being overcome with fear. I shall remember how St. Peter at a blast of wind began to sink because of his lack of faith, and I shall do as he did: call upon Christ and pray to him for help. And then I trust he shall place his holy hand on me and in the stormy seas hold me up from drowning."

Father,
    may the life of St. Thomas More give us
    the courage to proclaim our faith.

THE BIRTH OF   June 24
JOHN THE BAPTIST

THE BIRTHDAY of John the Baptist, six months before the birth of Jesus, has been celebrated on June

24 from the earliest days of the Church. Jesus himself called John, who prepared the way for him by his preaching, the greatest of men. A "voice in the desert," John, as the final prophet of the Old Testament, told the people of his time that their Lord was near.

The announcement of John's birth by the Angel Gabriel to Zachary, his father, was received with disbelief because Zachary's wife, Elizabeth, was beyond childbearing age. Yet the angel insisted, "You shall call his name John for he will be great before the Lord and filled with the Holy Spirit, even from his mother's womb."

In the wastelands of Judea, people from all ranks of society—soldiers and priests, tax collectors and workers—came to hear John and their hearts were moved by his call to repent. Many were baptized by him in the River Jordan as a sign of their conversion; some remained to live with him as his disciples. His denunciation of King Herod's immoral conduct shocked the king's court, and John eventually suffered death for speaking truth to the powerful.

Jesus began his own mission by being baptized by John. Recognizing the Son of God, whose "sandals he was not worthy to untie," John said, "He must increase, and I must decrease." John's life prepared for Jesus who was eternal life.

Early commentators never failed to note that after June 24, the feast of John the Baptist, the sun's light begins to decrease until December 25, the birth of Jesus, when the light of the sun increases again.

Lord, may you increase your life within us.

ST. CYRIL OF ALEXANDRIA   June 27
(370-444) bishop and doctor

ST. CYRIL was born in Alexandria, Egypt, in 370. His uncle, Theophilus, was the patriarch of Alexandria and died in 412. Upon his death, Cyril succeeded him as patriarch. It is thought that Cyril was present at the Synod of the Oak, a meeting at which St. John Chrysostom was deposed.

Cyril began to close the churches of the Novation heretics and had many confrontations with the Jews of the city. In 428, Nestorius became the Archbishop of Constantinople. He believed that Christ was two persons, one human and the other divine, and denied Mary the title, "Mother of God." Cyril's learning and deep faith prepared him to uphold the Catholic faith against Nestorius.

Cyril appealed to Pope Celestine I and had Nestorius condemned. At the third General Council of Ephesus in 431, Cyril acted as Pope Celestine's representative and presided over two hundred bishops. As a result of this conclave, Nestorius was condemned and excommunicated. Eventually, he was exiled to the deserts of Egypt. Cyril, a Doctor of the Church, died in 444.

His absolute loyalty to his faith offset the controversial traits of harshness and prejudice that weakened his personality. He produced a vast quantity of theological and spiritual works which nourished Christianity in later centuries.

Christ was not born as an ordinary man of the holy Virgin and then the Word descended upon him; the Word became flesh in her womb.

St. Cyril

ST. IRENAEUS June 28
(130-200) bishop and martyr

ST. IRENAEUS, one of the greatest theologians of the second century, was born in Smyrna, Asia Minor, in 130. He was a disciple of St. Polycarp, who was a companion of St. John the Apostle. Irenaeus always recalled the memory of his holy teachers and reported clearly all they said and did.

Polycarp sent him as a missionary to Lyons, and he became a priest under the Bishop of Lyons, St. Pothinus. He became one of the founders of the Church in France and was elected Bishop of Lyons in 178. He twice went to Rome to counsel Pope Eleutherius to be patient in the disputes between the Roman Church and the Montanists in Phrygia.

Irenaeus wrote extensively defending the Christian faith against the false teachings of the Gnostics, who were enticing Christians to join the ranks of their heresy. His most famous work is a five-book treatise, *Adversus omnes haereses*.

Fairly, courteously, and painstakingly, Irenaeus presented their doctrines in detail and showed how they differed from the teachings of Holy Scripture and the apostles. A patient teacher who respected those he dealt with, even his adversaries, he returned repeatedly to the simple yet profound belief of Christianity:

"From the beginning the Son teaches us about the Father. The Word revealed God to us and presented us to God. Our life is the glory of God. Our life is to see God."

He is said to have been martyred around the year 200.

Father,
  you called St. Irenaeus to uphold the faith.

ST. PETER (d. 64)   June 29
and
ST. PAUL (d. 64) apostles

A FEAST honoring these two great saints has been celebrated by the Roman Catholic Church since

the third century. There is sound evidence that both Sts. *Peter* and *Paul* preached in the city of Rome and were martyred there under the Emperor Nero about the year 64. The Church of Rome praises them as its founding apostles: "Peter, our leader in faith, and Paul, its fearless preacher. Peter raised up the Church from the faithful flock of Israel, Paul brought God's call to the nations." (Preface from the Mass)

Simon, a fisherman on the Sea of Galilee, was one of the first whom Jesus called to follow him. Changing his name to Peter, "Rock," the Lord promised to build his Church on him and gave him power in heaven and on earth. A natural spokesman for the other disciples, Peter called Jesus "the Christ, the Son of the living God."

When Jesus was arrested, Peter denied him three times and afterwards wept bitterly over his enormous betrayal of the one he promised to die for. When he rose from the dead, Jesus asked Peter three times if he loved him and, hearing the disciple's simple answer, "Yes, Lord, you know I love you," gave him again a privileged place at his side. "Come, follow me."

Filled with the Holy Spirit at Pentecost, Peter began to preach about Jesus Christ to the crowds in Jerusalem and Samaria and later made his way to Rome where he died a martyr's death as leader of that Church. Tradition says he died crucified head down, since he considered himself unworthy to die as his Lord had done.

Saul of Tarsus was a zealous Jew, a Pharisee, who after his dramatic conversion on the way to the city of Damascus became a fervent apostle of Jesus. After a three-year period in Arabia, where he assimilated his new faith, Paul journeyed to the cities of Damascus, Jerusalem, Antioch and then crisscrossed the cities of Asia Minor establishing communities of Christians among the gentiles. Because of his activity he suffered constant harrassment from his enemies, enduring shipwreck, imprisonment, and beatings. At the same time he was greatly loved by those Christians to whom he ministered; Corinthians, Ephesians, Galatians, Romans To them St. Paul wrote his powerful letters of consolation and instruction which the Church still reads today as inspired by God himself.

After imprisonment in Rome, he was beheaded along the Ostian Way where his burial place is still venerated. In his letter to Timothy he wrote, "The time has come for me to go. I have fought the good fight; I have run the race: I have kept the faith. Now I await the crown of justice which the Lord, the just judge, will give to me on that day, and not only to me but to all who long for his coming."

> *Father,*
> *through Sts. Peter and Paul*
> *your Church first received the faith.*

FIRST MARTYRS
OF THE CHURCH OF ROME

June 30
(d. 64)

IN THE year 64, Rome was devastated by a terrible fire. Many Romans thought that the Emperor Nero was responsible for the tragedy. In order to protect himself, Emperor Nero blamed the fire on the Christian community of Rome. Along with St. Peter, many other Christians suffered martyrdom during this persecution.

Some of the Christians were thrown to wild dogs, others crucified, and many were burned alive after being impaled on stakes. They were tortured unmercifully, and Pope Clement recalled in a letter the bravery and patience of those men, women and children, whom he knew himself and counted as founders of the Roman Church. To the people of his day he wrote: "We are placed in the same arena and the same contest lies before us. . . . Let us keep our eyes on the blood of Christ, realizing how precious it is to his Father, since it was shed for our salvation and brought the grace of repentance to the world."

Father, give us courage to stand firm
for the faith you have given us.

JULY

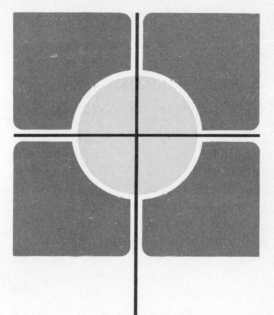

ST. THOMAS

July 3

(first century) apostle

ST. THOMAS, one of the twelve apostles, was a Jew from Galilee called by Jesus to accompany him on his mission to proclaim the Kingdom of God. When Jesus' life was threatened as he went to raise Lazarus from the dead, Thomas said to the others, "Let us also go, that we may die with him." At the Last Supper, when Jesus spoke of going away to his Father, Thomas replied, "Lord, we do not know where you are going, and how can we know the way?" With the rest of the apostles, Thomas fled when Jesus was arrested and put to death.

On Easter Sunday, Thomas was not with the others when Jesus came into the room where they were. Though they told him jubilantly, "We have seen the Lord!" Thomas answered, "I will not believe until I put my finger into the nail marks in his hands and his side." The expression, "doubting Thomas," comes from this incident.

One week later, when Jesus appeared again to his disciples, Thomas was with them. Jesus said, "Take your finger and examine my hands. Put your hand into my side. Do not remain an unbeliever. Believe!" Thomas said, "My Lord and my God!"

"The unbelief of Thomas has done more for our faith than the faith of the other disciples," St. Gregory the Great has said. Our doubts are answered by the demand of Thomas to know that Jesus' resurrection was real.

Thomas is said to have preached the Gospel to the people of India. He was martyred eight miles from Madras and buried at Mylapore, India. The date of his death is unknown.

Because you have seen me, Thomas, you have believed; blessed are they who have not seen me and yet believe.

ST. ELIZABETH OF PORTUGAL   July 4
   (1271-1336)

ST. ELIZABETH was born into the royal family of Aragon, in 1271. Her father was King Peter III of Aragon and her great aunt was St. Elizabeth of Hungary. At the age of twelve, she married King Denis of Portugal. They had two children, Alfonso and Constance. Despite her husband's infidelity, Elizabeth remained devoted to him and faithful to her life of prayer. She was attentive to the many needs of the poor and opened a hospital at Coîmbra, an orphanage for foundlings, and a home for women at Torres Novas. She was always involved in the cause of peace and often intervened to settle quarrels between warring factions of her family.

Her son, Alfonso, was rebellious and led an army against King Denis. Denis felt that Elizabeth was siding with Alfonso and banished her from the kingdom for a short time. After the death of King

Denis in 1325, Elizabeth became a Franciscan tertiary and went to live in the convent of the Poor Clares at Coîmbra. While there she gave up most of her wealth to care for the poor. In 1336, Elizabeth successfully mediated a dispute between her son, King Alfonso IV, and King Alfonso XI of Castile. She died at Estremoz, Portugal, on July 4, 1336.

Father, you called the peacemaker blessed,
give us the gift to bring peace.

ST. ANTHONY ZACCARIA   July 5
(1502-1539) priest

ST. ANTHONY ZACCARIA was born at Cremona, Italy, in 1502. His father died when he was eighteen and his mother became responsible for his spiritual awareness. He studied medicine at the University of Padua and received his degree in 1524. He returned to Cremona and began his practice. However, he soon realized that he was called to heal souls as well as bodies and was drawn to the priesthood. He was ordained in 1528 at the age of twenty-six.

After his ordination, Anthony went to Milan and joined the Confraternity of Eternal Wisdom. He founded a community of women known as the Angelicals. Anthony had great devotion to St. Paul the Apostle, whose spirit he wished to enkindle in both himself and the community of priests he founded in 1530. The community of priests are known as the Barnabites, or the Society of Clerics of St. Paul. He died at Cremona in 1539.

Lord Jesus, inspire us to imitate you
with the zeal of your holy apostles.

ST. MARIA GORETTI   July 6
(1890-1902) virgin and martyr

ST. MARIA GORETTI was born at Corinaldo, Italy, in 1890, into a poor family of farm laborers. Her father, Luigi, moved the family to Ferriere di Conca, not far from Nettuno in the Roman Campagna. Luigi Goretti died in 1896, and his wife had to work hard in the fields to support the family of six children.

On July 5, 1902, Maria was attacked in her home by eighteen-year-old Alexander Serenelli. Alexander was the son of her father's partner and lived in the Goretti's house. Maria, not quite twelve years old, was dragged into one of the bedrooms by Alexander. She resisted his advances and was stabbed repeatedly with a long dagger. Maria was rushed to the hospital, and as she lay dying, she prayed that Alexander would be forgiven and her family would be provided for. On July 6, 1902, after receiving viaticum, she died in the presence of her mother, two nuns, the parish priest of Nettuno, and a Spanish noblewoman.

Her death profoundly moved the people of Italy and stirred worldwide notice. Alexander was sentenced to thirty years in prison and remained unrepentant. One night, however, he had a dream of Maria gathering flowers and offering them to him. He became a changed man and was released from prison after twenty-seven years because of good conduct. Alexander Serenelli was alive when Maria was canonized on July 25, 1950, by Pope Pius XII.

> Lord God,
>> give us strength to do what is right
>> no matter what the cost.

ST. BENEDICT   July 11
(480-547) abbot

ST. BENEDICT, brother of St. Scholastica, was born at Nursia, Italy, in 480. His family was wealthy, and he was educated in Rome at a time when barbarian invasions and moral decline seriously threatened to destroy the city and the Roman empire. Disgusted with the moral decline of his companions and society in general, Benedict left Rome and lived in the village of Enfide for a number of years.

About 500, Benedict went to the wild and remote area of Subiaco. While there, he came under the tutelage of the monk, Romanus. Benedict became a monk and spent the next three years living a life of prayer and solitude in a cave. He began to attract many followers, and by 525, he had founded twelve monasteries in Subiaco.

In 529, after this was accomplished, Benedict left for Monte Cassino. Again, many disciples were drawn to him. In 530, he founded the great monastery at Monte Cassino which would become the focal point for Western monasticism. Benedict became the abbot of Monte Cassino and organized his companions into one monastic community. The Benedictine Rule inspired monastic life in the Western Church for centuries to come. Monasticism and its monasteries were instrumental in preserving Western civilization in modern Europe and the West. A wise spiritual leader and worker of miracles, Benedict's life and works profoundly affected the spirituality and life of the Church and Western civilization. He died at Monte Cassino on March 21, 1547.

Whatever work you begin to do, beg God in earnest prayer to make it perfect . . . We are going to establish a school for the Lord's service. Nothing harsh or burdensome will enter there, we hope . . . As we go forward in faith, our hearts will grow great, and we will run in the way of God's commandments with unspeakable love.

Rule of St. Benedict

ST. HENRY II
(973-1024) emperor

ST. HENRY II was born in 973 in Hildesheim, Bavaria, to Duke Henry of Bavaria and Gisella of Burgundy. He was educated by St. Wolfgang, Bishop of Ratisbon. In 955, he succeeded his father as the Duke of Bavaria. When his cousin, Otto III, died in 1002, Henry succeeded him as Emperor. In 1014, he was crowned Holy Roman Emperor by Pope Benedict VIII.

While he conducted the affairs of his government with great political skill, he nevertheless kept before his eyes the law of God and his responsibilities to the Church. The main concerns of Henry were the consolidation of power of the German monarchy and the reform of the Church. In 1004, he defeated Arduin of Ivrea by driving him out of Italy, and had himself crowned King of Italy. He also drove Boleslaus I of Poland out of Bohemia.

In 1006, Henry founded the See of Bamberg. Pope Benedict VIII consecrated the great Cathedral of Bamberg in 1020. Henry also established a monastery at Bamberg during this time. According to tradition, Henry went to Italy in 1021 on an expedition against the Greeks in Apulia. Along the way, he became ill and was cured by St. Benedict at Monte Cassino.

Henry saw that worthy bishops were appointed throughout his realm and respected the ecclesiastical reforms emanating from the great monastery at Cluny. He was a great friend of such famous monks as St. Odilo of Cluny and Richard of Saint-Vanne. Henry II died near Göttingen, Germany, in 1024 and is buried at the great cathedral in Bamberg.

> *Father, ruler of all,*
>> *give those who govern the nations of the world*
>> *a thirst for justice and truth.*

ST. CAMILLUS DE LELLIS   July 14
(1550-1614) priest

ST. CAMILLUS was born at Bocchianico, Italy, in 1550. A large man over six feet, six inches tall, he had an active, adventurous disposition. At the age of seventeen, he left home to go to war with the Venetians against the Turks, but he contracted a painful disease in his leg which left him hospitalized at the San Giacomo Hospital in Rome. He was an annoying patient, whom the hospital quickly dismissed. He was also a compulsive gambler, eventually losing all he had.

Down on his luck, Camillus began work in a Capuchin monastery at Manfredonia. One day, impressed by the words of advice someone spoke to him, he began to change. In 1576, he decided to serve the sick and returned to the hospital of San Giacomo in Rome, where he had been a patient.

His devotion and ability eventually won him the position as hospital superintendent.

Aware of the deplorable conditions in the hospitals of his time and the large number of unqualified personnel caring for the sick, Camillus gathered companions to devote themselves to his task. Through the intercession of his confessor, St. Philip Neri, Camillus was ordained a priest in 1584. He founded a new religious community, the Ministers of the Sick, or the Camellians, which ministered to victims of the plague, staffed hospitals, and nursed soldiers wounded in battle. When his companions accompanied troops fighting in Hungary and Croatia between 1595 and 1601, they became the first medical field unit. Camillus and his followers founded a new house in Naples in 1588, and Pope Gregory XIV officially recognized the congregation in 1591.

Despite multiple illnesses he suffered as he grew older, Camillus continued to nurse the sick himself, comforting those who suffered, and preparing the dying for their last journey. He resigned as superior of his order in 1607 and died at Rome on July 14, 1614. With St. John of God, he is patron of nurses and nursing associations.

Lord Jesus, you said, "I was sick and you visited me." May we see you in the sick and the suffering.

ST. BONAVENTURE   July 15
(1218-1274) bishop and doctor

ST. BONAVENTURE was born at Bagnorea, near Viterbo, Italy, in 1218. He became a Franciscan and studied at the University of Paris under a brilliant Englishman, Alexander of Hales. Bonaventure, also known as the "Seraphic Doctor," began an outstanding career as a teacher of theology and Holy Scripture at the University of Paris between 1248 and 1257. With St. Thomas Aquinas, his good friend, Bonaventure received his doctorate in theology in 1257 from the University of Paris.

That same year, Bonaventure was chosen minister general of the Franciscans. In 1265, Pope Clement IV wanted him to become Archbishop of York, but he declined. However, in 1273, Pope Gregory X appointed him Cardinal-Bishop of Albano.

Some of the great writings of St. Bonaventure are *Commentary on the Sentences, The Perils of the Last Times, Concerning the Poverty of Christ,* and *Concerning Perfection of Life.* Bonaventure not only enlightened the minds of those he taught, but also stirred their hearts. Though he searched into the depths of knowledge, he knew the importance of ordinary life. One becomes holy only by "doing common things well and being constantly faithful to small things." A constant joy seemed to fill this genuine follower of St. Francis. As he himself said, "Joy is the great sign of God's grace within the soul." He died while taking part in the Council of Lyons on July 15, 1274. St. Bonaventure is a Doctor of the Church.

Christ is the way and the door. Gaze on him hanging on the cross with your faith, hope, and love, wondering and joyful, grateful and filled with praise.

Then you will make Christ your 'pasch,' your passing over. Through the branches of the cross you will pass over the Red Sea, leaving Egypt and entering the desert. There you will taste the hidden manna and rest with Christ in the sepulcher, as if you were dead to things outside. You will experience, as much as one still living can, the promise made to the thief who hung beside Christ: Today you will be with me in paradise.

St. Bonaventure

OUR LADY
OF MOUNT CARMEL

July 16

THE PROPHET ELIJAH ascended Mount Carmel to pray for the heavens to open when the country around him was dry and without water. Finally, he saw a small cloud coming in from the sea bearing life-giving rain. In the twelfth century, Christian hermits came to live and pray on this mountain. In their vision, the cloud was a symbol of Mary, the Mother of God, who brought life to a parched world. They honored her under the title of Our Lady of Mount Carmel and later founded an order devoted to prayer under her patronage.

> Most beautiful Mother of God,
>   Splendor of heaven,
> You bring fruitfulness to the earth
>   and assist us in our needs.

> Star of the Sea, show yourself
>   a mother to me.
> Let the healing rain of your comfort
>   fall gently upon me.
> Hear my voice when I call.
> Mother of God,
> I place my cause in your hands. Amen.

ST. LAWRENCE OF BRINDISI   July 21
(1559-1619) priest and doctor

CESARE DE ROSSI was born at Brindisi, in the kingdom of Naples, in 1559. He was educated by the Conventual Franciscans in Brindisi and then by his uncle at the College of St. Mark in Venice. At the age of sixteen, he entered the Capuchin Franciscan Order at Verona. While there, he adopted the name of Lawrence. He studied philosophy and theology at the University of Padua. He was remarkably gifted in languages and was fluent in Greek,

Hebrew, German, Bohemian, French, and Spanish. He was a brilliant student and became an expert on the Bible. He was ordained about 1582.

In 1596, Lawrence became definitor general of the Capuchins in Rome, and Pope Clement VIII asked him to preach the Gospel and convert the Jews. He was also sent into Germany with Blessed Benedict of Urbino to work among the Lutherans. While there, he was instrumental in establishing friaries at Prague, Vienna, and Gorizea. Lawrence, at the request of Emperor Rudolph II, mobilized the German princes in an army to repel the Turks, who were about to invade Hungary. Because of his intervention, the Turks were defeated at the battle of Szekesfehevar in 1601. In 1602, he was elected minister general of the Capuchins.

Lawrence defended Catholicism in Germany and Austria by his writings and preaching. Emperor Rudolph asked him to go to Spain for the purpose of persuading King Philip III to join the Catholic League. While there, he founded a Capuchin house in Madrid. He retired to the friary at Caserta in 1618, but once again he was called upon to be a mediator. The leading citizens of Naples asked Lawrence to approach King Philip III of Spain and ask him to discipline and recall the Spanish viceroy, the Duke of Osuna. There was fear of tyranny, but Lawrence succeeded in having the Duke of Osuna recalled. He died in Lisbon after meeting with King Philip on July 22, 1619. He is a Doctor of the Church.

Lord, give us zeal for your truth
and strength to labor for your kingdom.

ST. MARY MAGDALENE
(first century)

ST. MARY MAGDALENE is one of the most appealing characters in the Gospels. Only a few details about her appear there, yet Christians know her as a woman of great love, desire, and unwavering loyalty. She was born at Magdala, near Tiberias, in Galilee.

Mary Magdalene stood beside Jesus while he was dying on the Cross. With Mary, his mother, and a few other disciples, she watched helplessly as the one she loved suffered through the dark hours of Good Friday. Then with the others she prepared his dead body for burial.

Early Easter morning, she returned anxiously to his tomb to complete the burial anointings, only to find his body gone. She began to weep. Through her tears she suddenly saw a man standing beside her whom she thought was the gardener. When he spoke her name, she knew he was Jesus, risen from the dead.

"Mary!" Jesus said to her. "Rabboni! Teacher!" Mary joyfully responded. Then Jesus spoke these mysterious words, "Do not cling to me, for I have not yet ascended to the Father."

We can see Jesus, not rejecting her at this joyous

moment, but readying her, who followed him so devotedly in life, for following him now in faith. Reach out and cling to me now by faith, he seems to say. Touch me with the hand of your faith; seek me with eyes of faith; run towards me with limbs of faith. Now I will never be far from you. I am forever in your heart.

"I have seen the Lord," Mary announced to Jesus' disciples. Her experiences of the Lord, in his ministry, in the desolate hours on Calvary, in the brightening hours of Easter morning, echo through the centuries to strengthen our faith. She loved much, and through her love she found the God she sought.

By the prayers and example of Mary Magdalene may we proclaim Christ as our Lord.

ST. BRIDGET OF SWEDEN   July 23
(1303-1373) religious

ST. BRIDGET was born in Sweden in 1303 to a wealthy and noble family. Her father was Birger Persson, governor of Upland, Sweden, and her mother was Ingeborg Bengtsdotter, daughter of the governor of East Gothland. Bridget's mother died when she was twelve and she was raised by her aunt at Aspenäs on Lake Sommen.

At the age of fourteen, she married Ulf Gudmarsson and had eight children, one of whom became St. Catherine of Sweden. In 1335, she was called to the court of King Magnus II and became the principal lady-in-waiting to Blanche of Namur, his new wife and the Queen of Sweden. In 1340, Gudmar, her youngest son, died and Bridget made a pilgrimage to the shrine of St. Olaf of Norway at Trondhjem.

Upon returning from her pilgrimage to the court of King Magnus, Bridget became discouraged with the wanton lifestyle of Magnus and Blanche. She was granted a leave of absence and went on a pilgrimage with her husband, Ulf, to Compostela. During their return voyage, Ulf was taken ill at Arras. After his recovery, Bridget and Ulf dedicated their lives to God and decided to live the monastic life. Ulf died in 1344 at the Cistercian monastery of Alvastra.

Bridget lived at Alvastra for the next four years and experienced many revelations. After a vision, she returned to the court of King Magnus and denounced his lifestyle. He repented for a short time and endowed her monastery at Vadstena, which was founded in 1344. It was at Vadstena that Bridget founded an order of nuns known as the Order of the Most Holy Savior, or the Bridgettines.

Bridget went to Rome in 1350 with the intention of returning Pope Clement VI from Avignon. While in Rome, she was concerned with the well-being of the poor and became well known for her prophecies and revelations. The foremost of her priorities were the reform of the Church and the return of the papacy to Rome from Avignon.

In 1371, Bridget made a pilgrimage to the Holy Land with her sons, Charles and Birger, and her daughter, Catherine. Upon her return from the pilgrimage, she died at Rome on July 23, 1373. She is the patroness of Sweden.

Glory to you, Father, Son, and Holy Spirit,
for the life you have given your people.

ST. JAMES (d 42) apostle

ST. JAMES, the brother of St. John the Apostle, was also known as St. James the Greater in order to distinguish himself from St. James the Less, who was younger. James, a fisherman by trade, was born at Bethsaida in Galilee. One day, he and John were fishing with their father, Zebedee, when they were approached by Jesus. Jesus called them to become his disciples and they obeyed. Leaving their fishing nets and father, Zebedee, behind, they accompanied Jesus on his mission.

Jesus called James and John "Sons of Thunder," because they were so energetic and impetuous. Once they were received poorly by a Samaritan town and they asked Jesus if he wanted to draw down fire from heaven upon the place. Jesus had to rebuke them.

James was with Peter and John at the raising of Jairus' daughter from the dead, witnessed the Transfiguration of Jesus, and accompanied Our Lord during the Agony in Gethsemane. Tradition says that he journeyed to Spain to preach the Gospel. He is honored today at the great shrine of Santiago de Compostela. He was the first of the apostles to die for Christ and was beheaded at Palestine in 42 by King Herod Agrippa I.

Lord, help us to drink from your cup of life,
to serve more than to be served,
to labor for the coming of your kingdom.

STS. JOACHIM and ANN   July 26
parents of Mary

ANCIENT CHRISTIAN tradition records the names of Sts. Joachim and Ann as the parents of Mary, the mother of Jesus. They were both members of the tribe of Judah of the house of David. According to tradition, Joachim and Ann came to Jerusalem from Galilee. Over the centuries, they have been honored, especially in the East, at great churches and shrines built in memory of them. Historically and biblically, not much is known of Joachim and Ann, except that they are the parents of Mary and grandparents of Jesus.

By their fruits we know how people lived, Jesus

taught. The Church recognizes the grandparents of Jesus as models of family virtue and faith, which they transmitted to their offspring.

> O good St. Ann,
>> Mother of Mary, grandmother of Jesus,
>> intercede before God for our families
>> and their children.
>> May one generation hand on to another
>> faith in God's promise and
>> trust that he will do great things
>> for those who reverence his name.

ST. MARTHA   July 29
   (first century)

ST. MARTHA, the sister of Mary and Lazarus, lived with them in Bethany. It is apparent that they were very friendly with Jesus and received him as a guest into their home frequently. On one occasion, Martha asked her sister, Mary, who was sitting at Jesus' feet, to help her prepare dinner. Jesus, feeling that Martha was too preoccupied with household chores, stated that Mary had chosen the better part.

A woman of practical concern and straightforward faith, Martha was rewarded for her simple hospitality and trust in the power of Jesus. While she served Jesus bodily food, she was fed within by the Holy Spirit. Beyond measure, God responds to those who quietly tend to others' needs.

Martha met and pleaded with Jesus, when her brother died and asked him to raise Lazarus from the dead. Jesus said, "I am the resurrection and the life; whoever believes in me, though he should die, will come to life; and whoever is alive and believes in me, will never die. Do you believe this?" Martha replied, "Yes, Lord, I have come to believe that you are the Messiah, the Son of God; He who is to come into the world." Martha's tears of grief were turned into cries of joy when Lazarus was called back to life from the tomb at Jesus' word. According to legend, Martha, Mary and Lazarus went to preach the Gospel in France after the death of Jesus. She is the patroness of cooks.

Lord, let our simple gifts serve you.
Bless those who come to our door.

ST. PETER CHRYSOLOGUS   July 30
(380-450) bishop and doctor

ST. PETER was born at Imola, Italy, in 380. Cornelius, Bishop of Imola, educated him and ordained him as a deacon. In 424, he was appointed Archbishop of Ravenna by Pope Sixtus III. As archbishop, Peter became a confidante of Emperor Valentinian III and Pope Leo the Great.

Peter was a staunch defender of the Catholic faith and fought to eradicate paganism from his see. He influenced the development of the Church through his careful administration and constant preaching. His reputation as a preacher caused him to be given the name Chrysologus, "a man of golden words." His sermons were always short, however, for he did not want to tire his listeners. At times, Peter would become speechless from excitement while preaching.

He advised the heretic, Eutyches, to accept the teachings of Rome in order to unify the Church. Eutyches had been condemned by the Council of Constantinople. Peter officiated at the funeral of St. Germanus of Auxerre in 448. He died at Imola on December 2, 450. He is a Doctor of the Church.

Open our ears, O Lord, to hear your word,
and our hearts to accept your truth.

ST. IGNATIUS LOYOLA   July 31
(1491-1556) priest

FOUNDER OF the Society of Jesus, St. Ignatius Loyola was born in the castle of Loyola at Azpeitia in Guipuzcoa, Spain, in 1491. His father, Don Beltran, was lord of Oñaz and Loyola and head of one of the most ancient and noble families of Spain. Ignatius, christened Iñigo, was the youngest of eleven children. He became a page at the court of King Ferdinand V of Aragon, and entered the military under the command of the Duke of Nagara.

In 1521, a cannon ball broke his right shin and tore open his left calf during the battle of Pamplona against France. After being wounded, he was returned to the family castle at Loyola to recuperate. While recovering, he read books about the life of Christ and the lives of the saints. He was so inspired by what he had read, that he decided to dedicate his life to Christ. After his recovery, Ignatius made a pilgrimage to the shrine of Our Lady at Montserrat. For the next two years, he spent time in Manresa, alternating between a pauper's hospice and a cave. It was during this two-year period of prayer and solitude that he began his great book *Spiritual Exercises*.

Ignatius left Manresa in 1523 and went to the Holy Land. He returned to Spain in 1524 and went to Barcelona to study Latin. In 1526, he entered the University of Alcala. He went to Paris in 1528 and in 1534, at the age of forty-three, received his master of arts degree. While Ignatius was a student in Paris, he became very friendly with six fellow divinity students, one of whom was St. Francis Xavier.

In 1534, Ignatius and his six companions took a vow of chastity and poverty in a chapel on Montmartre. They pledged to preach the Gospel in Palestine and to offer their services directly to Pope Paul III. This is considered to be the founding of the Society of Jesus, or the Jesuits, as they are commonly known.

In 1537, Ignatius and his companions, who now numbered nine, went to Venice and were ordained. As they could not go to the Holy Land, they made a trip to Rome to offer their services directly to Pope Paul III. Thus, the order was officially formed in 1537 and officially recognized by Pope Paul III in a papal bull on September 27, 1540.

Ignatius was chosen the first superior general, and the members of the order made their final vows in 1541. Ignatius spent the rest of his life in Rome, directing the activities of the Society of Jesus. His book, *Spiritual Exercises*, was published in 1548. He died in Rome on July 31, 1556.

Teach us, good Lord,
to serve you as you deserve;
to give and not to count the costs;
to fight and not to heed the wounds;
to toil and not to seek for rest;
to labor and not to ask for any reward,
except to know that we do your will;
through Jesus Christ, our Lord.

St. Ignatius Loyola

AUGUST

ST. ALPHONSUS LIGUORI   August 1
(1696-1787) bishop and doctor

ST. ALPHONSUS LIGUORI was born at Marianelli, near Naples, Italy, on September 21, 1696. He received his doctorate in law from the University of Naples when he was sixteen. He practiced law for eight years and left a brilliant legal practice in 1723 in order to devote his life to Jesus Christ. He was ordained in 1726 and preached the Gospel in and around Naples to the country people of his region, who were then largely ignorant of their religion.

In 1732, he moved to Scala and founded a religious community, the Congregation of the Most Holy Redeemer, also known as the Redemptorists. Essentially, the Redemptorists were dedicated to preaching God's word through missions, retreats, and other spiritual ministries. Unfortunately, the Redemptorists were plagued by internal dissension during their formative years. Alphonsus was elected superior in 1743, and Pope Benedict XIV officially recognized the congregation in 1749.

In 1762, he was appointed Bishop of Sant' Agata dei Goti and devoted himself to preaching, writing, and reforming the Church. Severely afflicted with ill health and rheumatism, Alphonsus was allowed to resign his bishopric in 1775. He moved to Nocera, but was again confronted with internal feuding amongst his congregation.

In 1780, he was deceived and signed a document which divided the congregation into two groups.

The king of Naples recognized the document and Alphonsus was replaced as superior. For the next eighteen months, he was tested continually and suffered terribly. He recovered, due to his deep faith, and died on August 1, 1787 at Nocera, Italy.

In his long career of preaching and writing, Alphonsus is most often remembered for his *Moral Theology*, *The Glories of Mary* and *Visits to the Blessed Sacrament*. He stressed the love of God, the Redeemer, and sought to help people serve God in their daily lives. At a time when the Church was threatened by the excessive rigorism of Jansenism, he wanted to present the Christian life as neither too hard nor too easy. He counseled balance and trust in God's grace and recognized the many circumstances that influence human decisions and moral thinking. With practical concern, Alphonsus also recommended a concrete plan of prayer and devotions as a means to holiness. He is a Doctor of the Church.

God has loved us from all eternity.
 So he says: Remember I first loved you.
 You had not come to be,
 nor did the world yet exist,
 but I loved you already.
 From all eternity I have loved you.

St. Alphonsus

ST. EUSEBIUS OF VERCELLI (d. 371) bishop

ST. EUSEBIUS was born on the island of Sardinia. His parents were Christians, and his father died when he was a young boy. He was brought to Rome by his mother, educated there, and ordained a lector. In 340, he was appointed the Bishop of Vercelli. His own holiness impressed his priests and people alike. It is noted that he is the first person in the West who combined the clerical and monastic life.

In 355, Eusebius was urged to attend the Council of Milan by Pope Liberius. A powerful defender of the Catholic faith, Eusebius withstood pressures put on him by both the Arian bishops at the council and Emperor Constantius to condemn Athanasius. Instead, he insisted that everyone present at the council sign and approve the Nicene Creed before any decision was made about Athanasius. Because of his position, Emperor Constantius exiled him to Scythopolis in Palestine. Eusebius was placed under the auspices of the Arian Bishop, Patrophilus. While in Scythopolis, he was humiliated and harassed by the Arians. Eventually, he went to Cappadocia and then to the Upper Thebaid in Egypt.

Emperor Constantius died in 361 and Eusebius went to Alexandria to confer with Athanasius. He attended the Council of Alexandria and went to Antioch. His travels then took him to Illyricum to combat Arianism. Eusebius returned to Vercelli in 363 and met St. Hilary of Poitiers. Together they staunchly defended the Church against the threat posed by the Arian Bishop of Milan, Auxentius. Eusebius died at Vercelli on August 1, 371.

Father, we believe in Jesus Christ,
true God and true man.

ST. JOHN VIANNEY
(1786-1859) priest

ST. JOHN VIANNEY was born at Dardilly, near Lyons, France, on May 3, 1786, a few years before the French Revolution. After shepherding cattle on his family farm, he decided to study for the priesthood. He was drafted into the army, but deserted in 1809. When amnesty was granted by Emperor Napoleon in March of 1810, he returned to Dardilly.

John was tonsured in 1811 and entered the seminary at Lyons in 1813. Despite his poor record at studies, he was finally ordained on August 12, 1815. He was assigned as a parish priest in 1817 to Ars-en-Dombes, a remote, sleepy town of 230 people. Undoubtedly, his bishop wished to place him where not too much would be expected of him. Little did he realize the miracles of grace that would occur there. In 1824, with the help of Catherine Lassagne and Benedicta Lardet, he opened a free school for girls. This school laid the foundation for the establishment of La Providence, a shelter for orphans and deserted children, in 1827.

Through the prayer, penance and simple, tireless preaching of their parish priest, the people of Ars experienced a great spiritual awakening. News of this holy priest spread to the surrounding areas and soon men and women from all over Europe began to flock to the tiny village for confession and advice. More than three hundred visitors a day approached him. During winter, he would spend up to twelve hours a day in the confessional, and up to sixteen hours a day during summer. The few words he spoke to each were enough; they heard from him what they needed to hear. For forty-two years the Cure' of Ars labored in his out-of-the-way parish until he died on August 4, 1859.

When we pray our small hearts are stretched beyond themselves to reach lovingly to God. Through prayer we see what heaven will be. Prayer is honey making everything sweet; like the sun it melts the cold snow of sorrow away.

St. John Vianney

DEDICATION
OF ST. MARY MAJOR

IN 431, after the Council of Ephesus, Pope Sixtus III built a basilica in Rome on the Esquiline Hill. St. Mary Major is the oldest church in Western Christendom dedicated in honor of Mary, the Mother of God.

> We praise you, Virgin Mother of God,
>   a wall of strength surrounding your people,
>   you crushed the serpent's head and
>   turned our ancient sorrow into joy
>   through Jesus Christ, your Son.
>
> Teach us to be truly wise,
>   strengthen all who call on you,
>   intercede for peace on earth. Amen.

THE TRANSFIGURATION
OF JESUS

THE DIVINITY of Christ was made manifest to Sts. Peter, James and John when Jesus appeared before them on Mount Tabor and his face and clothing shone radiantly. His appearance before the apostles was a confirmation to them of his relation to the Church and his role as the Son of God. A feast in honor of the Transfiguration has been celebrated in the Christian churches of the East since the fifth century. In the Middle Ages, as interest grew in the Holy Land and the various sites connected with the life of Jesus, this feast was established in the Western Roman Empire.

Lord Jesus Christ,
through your Transfiguration on the mount,
strengthen our hearts lest they be broken
by the scandal of the Cross.
Enlightened by your grace,
may we share in the brightness of your glory.

ST. SIXTUS II August 7
(d. 258)   pope and martyr
and COMPANIONS   martyrs

ST. SIXTUS II, who became Bishop of Rome in 257, was arrested by soldiers of the Emperor Valerian while celebrating the liturgy in the cemetery of St. Callistus. He was beheaded along with six deacons: Magnus, Vincent, Stephen, Januarius, Felicissimus, and Agapitus. The witness of his martyrdom on August 6, 258, inspired the early Church to live its faith more strongly.

Happy are they who suffer persecution
for justice's sake;
the kingdom of heaven is theirs.   Mt 5, 10

ST. CAJETAN
(1480-1547) priest

ST. CAJETAN was born at Vicenza, Italy, in 1480, to a wealthy family of the nobility. He received a doctorate in civil and canon law from Padua University in 1504. He returned to Vicenza and became a senator, but wanted to serve God. Cajetan went to Rome in 1506 and was ordained in 1516.

While in Rome, he refounded the Confraternity of the Divine Love, a devout and zealous congregation of priests. Upon returning to Vicenza in 1518, he entered the Oratory of St. Jerome and became involved with helping the incurable sick and with reforming society. He founded a similar oratory in Verona and went to Venice in 1520 to work in a hospital.

In 1523, Cajetan founded the Theatines in Rome with John Peter Caraffa, later Pope Paul IV, Paul Consiglieri and Boniface da Colle. When Rome was sacked by Emperor Charles V in 1527, the Theatines' house was destroyed and they escaped to Venice. Cajetan was elected superior in 1530 and resigned his title upon its expiration in 1533.

The Theatines, as well as Cajetan, were dedicated to works of charity, Church reform, and care of the poor. In order to relieve the poor in Naples who were being exploited by unscrupulous money lenders, Cajetan, with the help of Blessed John Marinoni, established a loaning organization, *montes pietatis,* to provide funds temporarily for those in need. He died at Naples on August 7, 1547.

> *Lord, you hear the cries of the poor;*
> *come to the aid of those in need.*

ST. DOMINIC
(1170-1221) priest

ST. DOMINIC was born at Calaruega, in Castile, Spain, in 1170. While a student in Palencia, he became a canon of the Cathedral of Orma. After his ordination, he joined the chapter, which adhered to the Rule of St. Augustine. In 1201, he became prior of the chapter.

In 1204, King Alfonso IX of Castile asked Bishop Diego d'Azevedo of Osma to marry his son in Denmark. Dominic accompanied the bishop, and during their journey through France they went through Languedoc where they were confronted with the heresy of the Albigenses, a group of heretical teachers who had become influential in certain parts of the country. While in Languedoc, Dominic met a man who was deeply confused by the Albigenses. Dominic spent the whole night in discussion with him and by daybreak the man was confirmed once again in his Catholic faith.

From this meeting, Dominic clearly saw his own mission: to preach the Gospel of Christ, battle the heresy of the Albigenses, and gather around him a group of holy and learned teachers who would instruct those in error. He remained in Languedoc for nearly ten years, preaching the word of God. In 1206, he founded a convent in Prouille.

In 1214, Dominic moved to Toulouse, received an endowment, and attended the Fourth Lateran Council in 1215. In 1216, Dominic gathered his sixteen companions in Prouille and adopted by-laws for his congregation, which became known as the Order of Preachers, or the Dominicans. These dedicated men and women combined learning with holiness and simplicity of life in their mission to spread the truth of Christ in the battle against the Albigenses. Pope Honorius III approved the congregation in 1216 and Toulouse became its headquarters.

Soon after, the friars were sent in all directions. Friaries would be established in Spain, France, England, and Italy. Dominic was appointed master general of the order in 1220 by Pope Honorius III and held the first general chapter of the order in Bologna that same year. He died at Bologna on August 6, 1221.

O God, send us your light and your truth.

ST. LAWRENCE
(d. 258) deacon and martyr

ST. LAWRENCE, a deacon of the Roman Church, went to his death four days after the martyrdom of Pope Sixtus during the persecution of the Emperor Valerian in the year 258.

According to tradition, Lawrence, aware that he was also to be martyred, began to distribute the monies and treasures of the Church to the city's poor. The Roman prefect, hearing about this, wanted the wealth for the government, so he promised Lawrence clemency, if he would show him where the Church's gold and silver were. Lawrence asked for three days to gather the treasure. Then he went through the city and invited all the poor and misfortunate supported by the Church to come together. When the prefect arrived, he saw the treasure of the Church: the blind, the maimed, the lepers, the orphans, and the old.

Angrily, the prefect ordered Lawrence to be burned alive. Witnesses described the saint cheerfully undergoing this dreadful death, even joking with his executioners. Many non-Christians were so moved by this event, according to tradition, that they converted. In fact, it is said that the entire city of Rome became Christian as a result of Lawrence's life and death. He was buried in the cemetery of Cyriaca on the Via Tiburtina where Constantine the Great built a basilica.

The blood of martyrs is the seed of Christians.
Tertullian

ST. CLARE
(1193-1253) virgin

August 11

ST. CLARE was born at Assisi, Italy, in 1193. When she was eighteen, St. Francis was preaching in Assisi and his words greatly inspired her. In 1212, on Palm Sunday, she ran away from home and went to Portiuncula, where Francis lived. He met her at the chapel of Our Lady of the Angels, cut off her hair, and gave her a sackcloth held together by a cord. She went to live in the Benedictine convent of St. Paul near Bastia.

Her family greatly objected, but their objections fell on deaf ears. Clare moved to a convent in Sant' Angelo di Panzo and was joined by her sister who was fifteen. In 1215, Clare, along with her sister, mother, and other companions, went to live in a convent associated with the Church of San Damiano, outside Assisi. Clare was appointed superior of the congregation by St. Francis, and this is considered to be the origin of the Poor Clares. In a short time, convents were opened in Italy, France, Germany, and Prague.

The Poor Clares adopted a severe life of poverty, silence and austerity. They did not own any prop-

183

erty or possessions and existed only on contributions. In 1228, Pope Gregory IX granted them the *privilegium paupertatis*, which excused them from having any material possessions.

Clare was superior of the order for over forty years. She died at the convent of San Damiano in 1253.

Set your mind before the mirror of eternity!
your soul before the brightness of glory!
your heart before the divine presence,
and be transformed totally into the image of God
through contemplation.

Then you too may feel what his friends feel
us they taste the hidden sweetness
God has kept from the beginning
for those who love him.

St. Clare

ST. PONTIAN (d. 235)   August 13
pope and martyr and
ST. HIPPOLYTUS
(d. 235) priest and martyr

ST. PONTIAN was elected Pope in 230, succeeding Pope Urban I. He convened a synod at Rome in 232 which condemned the theologian, Origen. Pope Pontian resigned his position in 235 and was banished to Sardinia during the persecution of Christians which was begun under Emperor Maximinus.

In Sardinia, he met **St. Hippolytus,** who had also been banished there by Emperor Maximinus. Hippolytus was a priest and also one of the great theologians of the third-century Church. Some of his great writings are *The Apostolic Tradition, A Refutation of All Heresies* and *Philosophoumena.* He was greatly opposed to heresy in the Church, especially Modalism and Sabellianism. Because of his orthodox views, he was elected as the first antipope in 217. He was severely opposed to Pope Callistus I and his successors, Popes Urban and Pontian. Hippolytus was reconciled to the Church by Pontian in Sardinia. They were both martyred there in 235 for their beliefs. Their bodies were returned to Rome and they were honored as martyrs.

> Lord, you made your saints loyal and
> faithful to you. Make us steadfast
> in our faith.

THE ASSUMPTION OF August 15
THE BLESSED VIRGIN MARY

ON NOVEMBER 1, 1950, Pope Pius XII declared the Assumption of the Blessed Mother a doctrine of faith. The taking up of the body and soul of the Mother of God into heaven was celebrated in Jerusalem as far back as the fifth century. Gradually, various churches of East and West made it part of their calendar.

> Rejoice with the Mother of God,
>   with angels and saints,
> and celebrate this great feast:
>   the Assumption of the Virgin Mary.
>
> On earth she was a fruitful virgin,
>   in heaven she intercedes for all;
> through this blessed woman,
>   the Spirit's gifts still flow upon us,
>   and her words teach gentle wisdom.
>
> At her assent the earth blossomed;
>   she sought good things for the poor.
> Now in heaven her care is undiminished,
>   near her Son she seeks the good of us all.

> adapted from a homily by Theothekno,
> Bishop of Palestine, +650

ST. STEPHEN OF HUNGARY   (969-1038)

August 16

ST. STEPHEN was born in Hungary in 969. He was baptized in 985 with his father, Geza, duke of the Magyars. Stephen married Gisela, the sister of Emperor Henry II, in 995. Upon his father's death in

997, Stephen succeeded Geza as duke of the Magyars.

After consolidating his power in Hungary, Stephen wished to Christianize the country. He sent St. Astrik to Rome in order to obtain Pope Silvester II's permission to Christianize Hungary and to have himself crowned king. Astrik, who became the first Archbishop of Hungary, returned from Rome with permission and a royal crown. In 1000, Stephen became King Stephen of Hungary.

Esztergon became the primatial see of Hungary, and Stephen dedicated himself to bringing his people to Christianity. He built many churches and monasteries and encouraged missionaries to preach the Gospel. He completed the monastery of St. Martin, which was begun by his father. He established a system of tithes so that the Church and the poor would be taken care of. Every tenth town had to build a church and support a pastor, and all pagan customs were eradicated. Stephen was also responsible for unifying the Magyars.

His son, Emeric, died in 1031 due to a hunting accident. With no direct heir to the throne, Stephen had to endure many confrontations within his family concerning succession. He died in 1038 and is buried at Szekesfehevar, Hungary.

King of heaven and earth,
inspire those who govern the nations to live in
justice and peace.

ST. JOHN EUDES
(1601-1680) priest

ST. JOHN EUDES was born at Ri, in Normandy, in 1601. At the age of fourteen, he entered the Jesuit college at Caen. He received his minor orders in 1621 and entered the Congregation of the Oratory of France in 1623. He was ordained in 1625 and went to work among the sufferers of the plague in Normandy. Soon after, he retired to the Oratory of Caen.

In 1631, another plague struck and John went out to work with the victims. He spent the next ten years giving missions as a parish missionary and hearing confessions throughout France. In 1641, with the help of Madeleine Lamy, he founded a home for penitent women, which was turned over to the Visitandine Order of Caen.

John left the Congregation of the Oratory in 1643 to establish the Congregation of Jesus and Mary, also known as the Eudists. He encountered opposition from the Jansenists and the French Oratorians, but persisted even though he could not receive approval from Rome. He also established the Sisters of Our Lady of Charity of the Refuge at Caen in 1650.

A noted spiritual writer, John wrote *The Devotion to the Adorable Heart of Jesus* and *The Admirable Heart of the Most Holy Mother of God.* He is credited with initiating devotions to the Sacred

Heart of Jesus and to the Heart of Mary. He died at Caen on August 19, 1680.

O God, you reveal yourself in the life of Jesus, your Son. Keep our eyes fixed on him.

ST. BERNARD
(1090-1153) abbot and doctor

ST. BERNARD was born at Fontaines, a castle near Dijon, France, in 1090. His was a wealthy and noble family and his father, Tescelin Sorrel, was a Burgundian noble. Bernard was well educated and sent to Châtillon on the Seine for a complete education among secular canons.

His mother, whom he loved dearly, died when Bernard was a young man. Deeply touched by her death and with a growing love of God, Bernard entered the Cistercians at Cîteaux in 1112. He was joined by thirty-one companions, including four of his brothers and an uncle. The abbot of Cîteaux, St. Stephen, sent Bernard with twelve companions, to establish a new monastery in the diocese of Langres in Champagne. In time, Bernard was chosen as the abbot of the monastery of Clairvaux, from which sixty-eight new monasteries were founded throughout Europe by the time of his death.

As a monk, Bernard worked tirelessly to strengthen religious life. His sermons and writings, especially *De Diligendo Deo* and *De consideratione*, describing the workings of God with the human soul, inspired the people of his time. They were the result of Bernard's own experience of God's grace in his life.

The needs of the Church and his society continually called this eloquent saint from his monastery. Popes, bishops, and princes sought his advice in matters of policy and politics. He always sought to keep the Christian faith uncompromised.

In the disputed papal election of 1130, Bernard supported Pope Innocent II against the claims of the antipope Anacletus II. In 1145, the papal legate, Cardinal Alberic, asked Bernard to go to Languedoc to preach against the heresy of the Albigenses.

In 1145, Pope Eugenius III, the successor to Pope Innocent II, had been the abbot of the Cistercian monastery of Tre Fontane. He asked Bernard to preach in France and Germany to generate enthusiasm for a Second Crusade. The Crusade was a failure and Bernard had to endure much criticism.

The hearts of men and women throughout Europe were stirred by the faith and eloquence of this dynamic saint. His great prayers to Mary, the Mother of God—for example, his *"Memorare"*—are witness to his strong devotion to her as well as her Son. He died at Clairvaux on August 20, 1153. Bernard is a Doctor of the Church.

Lord, what will you have me do? Here is the sign of a perfect spirit. Someone who leaves aside his or her own will so that they no longer seek or desire to do what they want, but only what God wills.

St. Bernard

ST. PIUS X   August 21
(1835-1914) pope

GIUSEPPE MELCHIORRE SARTO was born at Riese, in Venetia, Italy, on June 2, 1835. His family was very poor and he was the second of ten children. He entered the seminary at Padua and was ordained in 1858 at the age of twenty-three. He devoted the next seventeen years of his life to the pastoral ministry. Appointed Canon of Treviso in 1875, he became the Bishop of Mantua in 1884. In 1892, he was appointed Cardinal and Patriarch of Venice by Pope Leo XIII.

On August 4, 1903, Cardinal Sarto was elected to succeed Pope Leo XIII, who had died. As Pope Pius X, his great desire was to "restore all things in Christ." In 1905, he defied the government of France and defended the separation of Church and state. He forbade any civil power from interfering in a papal election. Pope Pius is known for his battle against purging "Modernism" from the Church. He also encourged daily reading of the Bible and frequent, if not daily, reception of communion—especially by children.

Pius X fought against errors that threatened the faith, urged Christians to take a greater part in social affairs and politics, and worked to reform the liturgical life of the Church. He sought justice and the rightful place of religion in his dealings with world governments and institutions. With deep concern, he labored for peace in a world being plunged into war. World War I began on August 4, 1914—Pius X died on August 20, 1914. He was canonized on May 29, 1954, by Pope Pius XII, the first pope to be so honored since Pius V in 1672.

O God, all things belong to you;
bless and restore in Christ our world.

THE QUEENSHIP OF MARY   August 22

FOLLOWING THE feast of Mary's Assumption into heaven on August 15, the feast of her Queenship celebrates her place among the angels and saints as the Queen of heaven and earth.

Hail, holy Queen, mother of mercy,
our life, our sweetness, and our hope.
To you do we cry,
poor banished children of Eve.
To you do we send up our sighs,

mourning and weeping in this vale of tears.
Turn then, most gracious advocate,
your eyes of mercy toward us,
and after this our exile
show us the blessed fruit of your womb, Jesus.
O clement, O loving,
O sweet Virgin Mary.

ST. ROSE OF LIMA   August 23
(1586-1617) virgin

ST. ROSE was born at Lima, Peru, in 1586. She was confirmed by St. Turibius, Archbishop of Lima, and took the name Rose, as Isabel was her baptismal name. Despite objections from her parents and friends, Rose admired St. Catherine of Siena, and was attracted to a life of prayer and reflection.

Her parents fell on hard times and Rose worked in the garden all day and sewed at night. She was very happy with this way of life, but her parents wanted her to marry. She refused their wishes, took a vow of virginity, and entered the Third Order of St. Dominic at the age of twenty. She became a recluse and lived in a small hut in the garden. She even went so far as to wear a thin crown of silver lined with sharp studs, a modern-day crown of thorns.

Rose cared for poor children, slaves, Indians and elderly people in an infirmary she set up in her family home. This is considered to be the beginning of social services in Peru. She spent the last three years of her life in the home of Don Gonzalo de Massa, a government official. Rose died there on August 24, 1617, and is the patroness of Peru and South America. She is also the first canonized saint of the Americas.

> O God, those who seek you
>   wholeheartedly, find you.
>   Help us to give ourselves to your service.

ST. BARTHOLOMEW   August 24
  (first century) apostle

ST. BARTHOLOMEW, one of the twelve apostles, was born in Galilee and is probably the same person as Nathaniel, whom Philip brought to see Jesus of Nazareth. "Can anything good come from that place?," Nathaniel asked. (John 1, 45-51)

Jesus called him an Israelite incapable of deceit, an honest, straightforward man, and promised that heaven would open for him and the mysteries of God would be revealed before his eyes.

Like some other apostles, little is known about St. Bartholomew's activity after Pentecost. According to some reports, he preached the Gospel in Armenia and India and was beaten and beheaded by King Astyages for his faith in Christ.

> *Lord, keep strong the faith*
> *which made Bartholomew believe in*
> *your Son.*
> *May we too witness to what we believe*
> *wherever we go.*

ST. LOUIS OF FRANCE   August 25
(1214-1270)

ST. LOUIS was born in Poissy, France, on April 25, 1214. He was the son of King Louis VIII and Blanche, daughter of Alfonso of Castile and Eleanor of England. King Louis VIII died when Louis was twelve years old, and his mother became regent for him. At the age of nineteen, he married Margaret, the eldest daughter of Raymund Berenger, Count of Provence. They had eleven children, five sons and six daughters. In 1235, Louis came of age and took over the government of France. Devoted to God and his people, he was a model ruler who promoted peace and justice in his kingdom. He cared for the poor, founded hospitals, promoted learning, and lived humbly and prayerfully among his people. The system of justice he established settled disputes among his subjects by just procedures rather than violence or fraud.

Louis defeated King Henry II of England at

Taillebourg in 1242 and made a treaty with him in 1259. At the same time, his devotion to Christ inspired him to lead a Crusade to the East in 1248. Louis captured Damietta in Egypt, but in 1250 was captured and taken prisoner by the Saracens. He was eventually released and with his army sailed to Palestine, where he remained until 1254. He returned to France in 1254 upon hearing of the death of his mother, who had been acting as regent during his absence.

Louis announced another Crusade in 1267 and left for the East in 1270. During the voyage, he became ill with typhus and died at Tunis, on August 25, 1270. Though his two Crusades into the Holy Land largely failed, his heroic example and loyalty to his army left a lasting memory for his successors and his people. He is one of the patrons of France.

God of power and might,
bring justice and peace to the nations.

ST. JOSEPH CALASANZ   August 25
(1557-1648) priest

ST. JOSEPH was born at Peralta de la Sal, Aragon, Spain, on September 11, 1557. After being ordained in 1583 and appointed vicar general of Trempe, he went to Rome in 1592. Five years later, with the help of two priests, he founded the first free school in Europe for the education of poor children. Supported by Pope Clement VIII and Pope Paul V, Joseph opened other schools in Italy, Spain, Bohemia and Poland. In 1621, the congregation was officially recognized as a religious order, the Clerks Regular of Religious Schools, or the Piarists, and Joseph was elected superior general.

Joseph hoped to establish a system of primary and secondary schools and wanted children to love goodness. A friend of Galileo, the scientist, Joseph suffered from great trials and misunderstandings later in his life. His reputation was questioned by Fr. Sozzi and Fr. Cherubini, fellow members of the congregation, who succeeded him as superior general of the order. In 1646, Pope Innocent X dissolved the congregation, but Joseph patiently persevered in his mission that the young be educated for the future. He died at Rome on August 25, 1648. The Piarists were restored as a religious order in 1669. Joseph is one of the patrons of Christian schools.

*God, give us patience for doing
what you give us to do.*

ST. MONICA   August 27
(332-387)

ST. MONICA, the mother of St. Augustine, was born in Tagaste, North Africa, about 332. Married to a pagan, Patricius, she had three children, two sons and a daughter. Because she recognized his extraordinary gifts, she tried to give Augustine the best education possible. Above all, she wanted him to use his gifts for God and the Catholic faith. Through her efforts, Patricius was converted to Christianity in 370. He died one year later.

Augustine disappointed her by chosing a life of pleasure, accepting the Manichaean heresy, and rejecting Christianity. Turning to God, Monica spent herself in earnest prayer for her wayward son. A priest whose advice she sought said to her, "It is not possible that the son of so many tears should perish."

Monica followed her son to Rome in 383 and then to Milan in 386. There she learned he was converted to Christianity. She joined him in preparing for his baptism by St. Ambrose on Easter, 387. As they were returning to Africa, Monica fell mortally ill at the seaport of Ostia. Augustine tells of her moving words of farewell before she died. "Son, nothing in this world now makes me happy. All my hopes have been fulfilled. All I wished to live for was that I might see you a Catholic and a child of heaven. God has given me more: I see you ready to give up everything and become his servant." She died in 387.

Lord,
the tears of St. Monica moved you to convert her son, St. Augustine.

ST. AUGUSTINE   August 28
(354-430) bishop and doctor

ONE OF the great Christian teachers of all time, St. Augustine was born at Tagaste, North Africa, on November 13, 354. His father, Patricius, was a pagan and his mother was St. Monica. Patricius was converted to Christianity in 370 and died one year later.

Augustine went to Carthage in 370 to study rhetoric and philosophy. While there, he met a woman with whom he would have a relationship until 385. She bore him a son, Adeodatus. He was deeply attracted to Manichaeism, but became disillusioned after meeting Faustus, the leading Manichaean teacher of that time. He left for Rome in 383 and opened a school of rhetoric. Disturbed with his surroundings, he went to Milan in 384 and accepted a post as master of rhetoric.

Augustine thirsted for wisdom. He found what he was seeking as he listened to the preaching of St. Ambrose in Milan. Augustine describes his spiritual journey in his *Confessions*, which recall his great struggle with evil and sin and his final experience of God's guiding grace. "Late have I loved you, O Beauty ever ancient, O Beauty ever new!" Augustine's later life echoes with grateful praise for the God he discovered to be so good.

Monica followed him to Milan in 386 and was present at his baptism by St. Ambrose on Easter in 387. After his baptism, Augustine deepened his own understanding of Christianity in the company of some friends, With Monica and several others, he went to Ostia in 387. Monica died there in November of 387 and Augustine returned to Rome.

In 388, Augustine returned to Tagaste, where he remained for three years. He was ordained in 391 as an assistant to Bishop Valerius of Hippo. He established a monastery in Hippo and staunchly defended the faith against Manichaeism and Donatism. He was consecrated bishop as coadjutor to Valerius in 395 and succeeded him in 396.

Augustine remained in Hippo for thirty-five years, preaching and writing. The most famous of his works are *Of the City of God* and *Confessions*. He engaged in controversy, received innumerable visitors seeking his counsel, and traveled to distant cities as a spokeman for the Christian faith. Not only the people of his time, but later generations as well, would find him a brilliant teacher of the Gospel proclaimed by Jesus Christ. He died at Hippo on August 28, 430 and is a Doctor of the Church.

O God, to turn from you is to fall,
to turn to you is to rise,
and to stand with you is to abide forever.

Grant us help in all we do,
guidance in all our confusion,
protection in all our dangers,
and a place in all our sorrows;
through Jesus Christ, our Lord.

St. Augustine

THE BEHEADING OF
ST. JOHN THE BAPTIST

August 29

(first century) martyr

ST. JOHN was born at Ain-Karim, near Jerusalem.
His father was Zachary, a priest in Jerusalem, and
his mother was Elizabeth, a kinswoman of the Virgin Mary. He lived as a hermit in the desert of Judea
until 27. He began to preach along the banks of the
Jordan River and stated, "Repent, for the Kingdom
of Heaven is at hand." Many people came to hear
him, including several who would become Christ's
apostles. It was John who baptized Jesus and
pointed him out as "the Lamb of God who takes
away the sins of the world." After the baptism, John
continued to preach along the banks of the Jordan.

The Gospel of Mark records the circumstances
of John the Baptist's death. Herod had John imprisoned because the Baptist had condemned the ruler's marriage to Herodias, his brother's wife. Infuriated with John, Herodias plotted to kill him. At a
birthday banquet, Herod, delighted by the dancing
of Herodias' daughter, told her he would give her
anything she requested. At her mother's prompt-
ing, she told him, "I want you to give me the head of
John the Baptist, here and now, on a dish."

John's death is celebrated by a feast, because it
resembles in so many ways the death of Jesus. Like
his master, John went to death silently and helplessly, a victim of petty revenge, human cowardice
and cruelty. His death in such absurd circum-

stances was his confession of faith in God, who alone sustains the human heart when it seems crushed by evil and injustice.

> *O God, make us faithful to truth and justice,*
> *as you did your servant, John the Baptist,*
> *herald of your Son's birth and death.*

SEPTEMBER

ST. GREGORY
THE GREAT

September 3

(540-604) pope and doctor

ST. GREGORY was born in Rome in 540. His family was one of the few patrician families left in Rome after the ravages of the preceding century, and his father, Gordian, was a wealthy man who owned property in Rome and Sicily. He was educated in Rome and became a public official. In 570, at the age of thirty, Gregory became the prefect of Rome. Though he was an honest and successful public servant and one of the richest men in Rome, he gave up his position of prominence to devote his life to God.

In 575, he converted his home into a monastery under the patronage of St. Andrew and the guidance of the monk, Valentius. He became a monk himself and established six more monasteries in Sicily. He was ordained by Pope Pelagius II and appointed papal ambassador to Constantinople in 579. In 586, he returned to Rome and became abbot of St. Andrew's monastery. After Pope Pelagius died of the plague in 590, Gregory was elected to the papacy, the first monk to be so honored.

Rome and the rest of Italy were being devastated by drought, famine, plague, and the fierce Lombard invaders. "What happiness is there left in the world?" Gregory asked in a sermon. "Everywhere we hear groans; our cities are destroyed, our land is a desert. See how Rome, the mistress of the world, has fallen." In 593, he negotiated a treaty with the

Lombard king, Agilulf. Through negotiations and alliances with the Lombards, Franks and Visigoths, he strengthened the Church's position in Italy, France and Spain. At the same time, he continued to spread the Gospel to the ends of the earth, sending missionaries to England and other parts of Europe.

Gregory conceived of his English mission, according to a story, one day when he saw some young English slaves in the marketplace. "Who are you?" he asked. "We are called Angels," they replied. "Angels of God," the pope answered. In 596, Gregory sent forty monks headed by St. Augustine to bring Christianity to England.

Through the fourteen tumultuous years of his papacy, Gregory suffered from a chronic illness that left him bedridden for long periods of time. Yet, he continued his tireless service to the Church, and in his preaching and writing urged the people of his day to a courageous patience in their trials. He called himself "the servant of the servants of God," a title every pope since has adopted. He died in Rome on March 12, 604. He is one of the four great Latin Doctors of the Church, along with Sts. Augustine, Ambrose and Jerome.

Lord, give us courage and patience
to serve you generously all our days.

THE BIRTH OF MARY   September 8

ALONG WITH the birth of Jesus and St. John the Baptist, Mary's birth has been celebrated by the Church from early times. In fourth-century Jerusalem a feast of her birth was celebrated at the Church of St. Ann, probably inspiring the Church of Rome also to celebrate too, this event. Mary's birth is seen always as part of God's plan for the salvation of the world through Jesus Christ.

> O Mary, you are blessed,
>   for the mysteries of the prophets
>   are fulfilled in you
>
> You were in the burning bush
>   and in the cloud that Moses saw;
> You were on the ladder rising up to heaven
>   that Ezechiel saw;
> You were in the ark of the covenant,
>   that David saw.
>
> At your birth these mysteries
>   are fulfilled.
>
> Glory to the Father, who sent his
>   only Son through you.
>
>   Adapted from an early Syrian text

ST. PETER CLAVER September 9
(1580-1654) priest

ST. PETER CLAVER was born at Verdu, in Catalonia, Spain, in 1580. He was educated at the University of Barcelona and decided to enter the Society of Jesus. He entered the novitiate of Tarragona in 1601 and was sent to the College of Montesione at Palma in Majorca. While there, he came under the tutelage of St. Alphonsus Rodriguez and requested to be sent as a missionary to the New World to minister to the neglected.

He went to Cartagena, in Colombia, South America, in 1610 and was ordained there in 1615. Peter worked with Fr. Alfonso de Sandoval, a great missionary among the black slaves, and declared himself "the slave of the blacks forever." Cartagena was one of the principal centers of the slave trade, and nearly one thousand slaves passed through its port every month.

Peter spent almost forty years serving the black slaves who came on slave ships to Cartagena before being sent to work at the plantations and mines in the area. It is said that he baptized nearly 300,000 slaves during his years in Cartagena. He brought food, clothing and encouragement to these poor people in their inhuman confinement and squalid conditions. Many were instructed in the Catholic faith, and Peter never turned away from their suffering or the revolting conditions of their captivity. He died at Cartagena on September 8, 1654, and the entire city, along with its slave population, mourned his passing. In 1896, Pope Leo XIII declared him the patron of all missionary work among blacks.

Lord, forgive our prejudices against others, and free those unjustly held captive.

ST. JOHN CHRYSOSTOM   September 13
(349-407) bishop and doctor

ST. JOHN CHRYSOSTOM was born at Antioch, Syria, in 349. He was the son of Secundus, a commander in the imperial army, and Anthusa, a devout Christian. His father died when he was an infant, and John was raised by his widowed mother, who gave him her deep faith and saw to it that he had a good education in law. He studied rhetoric under Libanius, the most famous orator of that era.

John was not baptized until he was twenty, as it was customary then to postpone baptism. In 374, after his mother's death, he joined a group of monks in the mountains south of Antioch to strengthen his spiritual life. Falling ill, however, he returned to Antioch in 381 and was ordained by Bishop Flavian in 386. His sermons stirred the people of that region.

In 398, John was named Archbishop of Constantinople, the most powerful city in the world. Generously providing for the poor and the sick, he reminded the wealthy and the privileged of their responsibilities to those less fortunate. Fearlessly he spoke out against injustice, even when it was found in the emperor's court. His eloquence brought him the name "Chrysostom," meaning "golden voice." In simple, everyday language, this sower of God's word cast the seeds of truth upon the world of his day.

John offended Emperor Arcadius and Theophilus, Archbishop of Alexandria. In 403, at the Synod of the Oak, John was condemned and exiled. He was recalled and banished to Cucusus, Armenia in 404 by Emperor Arcadius. For reasons of security, Arcadius ordered him to Pityus, at the far end of the Black Sea, in 407. He died along the way at Comana, Cappadocia, on September 14, 407. John described his banishment in these courageous words:

"Storms are all about me, yet I do not fear, for I stand on a rock. The roaring sea and the rising waves cannot dash into pieces the ship of Jesus Christ. I do not fear death, which brings me gain, nor banishment, for the Lord is everywhere; nor the loss of goods, for I came into this world naked and can take nothing out of it."

His last words were, "Glory to God for all things." St. John is one of the great Doctors of the Church.

Glory to God for all things.

THE TRIUMPH
OF THE HOLY CROSS

ST. PAUL the Apostle spoke of the power of Christ's Cross. According to tradition, the Empress Helena discovered the Lord's Cross in Jerusalem on September 14, 320. Five years later, a great church was built on Mount Calvary by Emperor Constantine to shelter the holy relic. Parts of the wood of the Cross were sent to the major cities of Christendom, where they were shown to the faithful on this special feast.

> *We worship you, O Christ,*
> *and we praise you, because by your*
> *Cross you have redeemed the world.*
>
> *By this holy tree*
> *you gave your people victory,*
> *and put aside the tree of our defeat.*

OUR LADY OF SORROWS   September 15

THE FEAST, popular in the Middle Ages, follows the feast of Mary's birth on September 8. It recalls the special bond between Jesus and Mary and reminds us of the torment and suffering of Christ. Mary suffered greatly as the Mother of God, and the pain she felt was real. The feast of Our Lady of Sorrows recalls the succession of sorrows Mary experienced during her life: the prophecy she heard from Simeon in the temple, the flight into Egypt, the three-day loss of Jesus on the pilgrimage to Jerusalem, meeting Jesus on the way to Calvary, the hours she stood beneath the Cross, the removal of Jesus from the Cross, and the burial of Jesus in a tomb.

> *Holy Mother, pierce me through;*
> *In my heart each wound renew*
> *of my Savior crucified.*

ST. CORNELIUS (d. 253)   September 16
pope and martyr
ST. CYPRIAN (210-258) bishop and martyr

STS. CORNELIUS and Cyrian lived together through a series of persecutions by the Roman government and together tried to keep their Christian communities from being split by dissension.

Cornelius was elected pope in 251 after a violent persecution of Christians in Rome by the Emperor Decius. A number of Christians there and in Africa renounced their faith rather than face death or imprisonment, and when peaceful times returned, they wished to return to their Church. Some in the Roman Church, led by Novatian, held that these lapsed Christians could never be reconciled. Cornelius and Cyprian opposed this severe position and maintained that God's forgiveness could not be limited. Their position prevailed. Cornelius died in exile at Civita Veccia in 253. He was buried in the cemetery of St. Callistus.

St. Cyprian was born at Carthage in 210. He was converted to Christianity in 246, ordained, and elected Bishop of Carthage in 248. A learned bishop, he enjoyed the love and respect of his people. In 249, during the Decian persecution, he fled into hiding but kept in contact with his diocese by frequent letters.

Decian died in 251 and Cyprian returned to Carthage. With Cornelius, he severely opposed the position of Novation concerning apostacy. Finally, in the new persecution under the Emperor Valerian in 258, Cyprian was seized, exiled and brought before the Roman proconsul, Galerius Maximus.

"The Emperor orders you to offer sacrifice," the proconsul said. "I will not sacrifice," Cyprian answered. "Think about it," the proconsul went on. "Do what you have to; there is no reason to think over what is so clear to me," Cyprian firmly responded.

He was beheaded by soldiers at Curubis on September 14, 258.

Heavenly Father, teacher of harmony and peace,
keep all of us true to your name
and help us live as one,
through Jesus, our Lord.

ST. ROBERT BELLARMINE

(1542-1621) bishop and doctor

ST. ROBERT was born at Montepulciano, Tuscany, Italy, on October 4, 1542. His family was very influential, and over their objections he joined the Society of Jesus in 1560. One of the leading theologians of his day, Robert was ordained at Ghent, Belgium, in 1570. After his ordination, he became the first Jesuit professor at Louvain in Belgium. He went to Rome in 1576 and was appointed to the chair of controversial theology at the Roman College. He became rector of the Roman College in 1592 and provincial of the Naples province of Jesuits in 1594. Appointed theologian to Pope Clement VIII in 1597, Robert became a cardinal in 1599 and Archbishop of Capua from 1602 to 1605.

Popes Clement VIII and Paul V sought Robert's advice and his learning in the controversies between the Catholic Church and the Protestant Reformers. He was fair and just in representing the position of his adversaries, but angered King James I of England and the Scottish jurist, William Barclay, because he denied the divine-right-of-kings theory. Robert was a staunch defender of both the Church and the papacy.

His two catechisms and books of theology and spirituality, namely *Disputations on the Controversies*, nourished the faith of many of his contemporaries, as well as generations that came after them. In 1610, Robert had to mediate in the affairs of his good friend, Galileo. He was able to convince Galileo to propose his theories of Copernicus as hypotheses rather than proven fact. Robert died in Rome on September 17, 1621. He is a Doctor of the Church.

> *Lord, help us to speak as you wish,*
> *and give us understanding of your ways.*

ST. JANUARIUS   September 19
(d. 305) bishop and martyr

ST. JANUARIUS was born in either Naples or Benevento, Italy, about 275. He was the Bishop of Benevento and was martyred with six companions at Pozzuoli during the persecution of Christians begun under Emperor Diocletian. He was arrested along with his deacon, Festus, and a lector, Desiderius, on the orders of the governor of Campania, Dracontius. The other companions were: Sossus, Proculus, Euticius and Acutius.

After Januarius was condemned to death by Diocletian, he and his companions were thrown to the lions in Pozzuoli. When the lions would not attack them, they were beheaded in 305. In the Cathedral of Naples, there is a glass vial which contains the dried blood of Januarius. It is said that when the relic is shown in public, eighteen times a year, the blood liquifies and bubbles. There is no medical or scientific explanation for this phenomenon and many people believe it is a miracle.

Lord, help us to follow you.

ST. MATTHEW September 21
(first century) apostle and evangelist

THE CALL of St. Matthew, the tax collector, to be one of the twelve apostles of Jesus is described in the Gospel which bears his name. "Jesus saw a man named Matthew at his post where taxes were collected. He said to him, 'Follow me!' And Matthew got up and followed him."

It is hard to imagine a more unlikely person for Jesus to call as a companion than Matthew. Tax collectors, as agents of a hated Roman government and members of a profession known for unfairness and greed, were despised by the Jewish people. They were excluded from the synagogue and the temple. No good Jew would have anything to do with them.

When Jesus invited Matthew to follow him and then ate at his house where Matthew's friends, outsiders like himself, were gathered, he heard the outraged comments of Capernaum's local leaders. "Why does he eat with tax collectors and sinners?" Jesus answered simply, "Those who are well have no need of a doctor; sick people do."

By calling Matthew, Jesus invited an outcast to enjoy the healing friendship of God. In a lesson of love, he showed that God wants all, no matter who they are, to share his life.

According to tradition, Matthew wrote down the stories and words of Jesus in Aramaic, the ancient language of Palestine. The first Gospel had its origins in him. Among the evangelists he is symbolized by the figure of a man, because Matthew's Gospel begins with the human origins of Jesus. There are reports that Matthew left Judea and preached in the East, where he was martyred in Ethiopia.

O God, may we follow your call.

ST. COSMAS   September 26
and
ST. DAMIAN   (d. 303) martyrs

ACCORDING TO tradition, Sts. Cosmas and Damian were twin brothers born in Arabia. They were doctors who lived at Aegeae, Cilicia, and ministered to the sick. Because they would not accept money for their services, they became known as "the holy moneyless ones."

They were arrested during the persecution of Christians under Emperor Diocletian. They were tried by Lysias, governor of Cilicia, tortured and beheaded in 303. They are buried at Cyrrhus, Syria, and many people have been cured after praying at their shrine.

> *Lord, cure the sick and suffering,*
>   *comfort those in pain.*

ST. VINCENT DE PAUL — September 27
(1581-1660) priest

ST. VINCENT was born in Pouy, France, on April 24, 1581. His family were French peasants and lived on a farm in Pouy. His father, Jean, recognizing his son's talents, resolved to give him a good education. Vincent attended the College of Dax and was educated by the Franciscan Recollects. He entered the University of Toulouse in 1596 to study theology and philosophy and was ordained there in 1600. Ambitious for a good comfortable position, he became one of the chaplains for Queen Margaret of Valois and tutored the children of the Count of Gondi.

Vincent came under the influence of Fr. Peter de Bérulle and his life changed. In 1617, while in the country, he heard the confession of a poor peasant and suddenly realized how badly the poor of France were being cared for. Resolving to give his life to serving the poor, he left the home of the Count and Countess of Gondi and began to work

among prisoners and galley slaves, who suffered from deplorable conditions. He was officially appointed chaplain of the galley slaves in 1619.

He gathered companions, and in 1625, founded the Congregation of the Mission, or the Vincentians, as they are commonly known, to preach the Gospel to the poor and work for the education of the clergy. With St. Louise de Marillac, he established the Sisters of Charity in 1633 to care for the sick, the orphaned, and the aged. Through his inspiration, many of the wealthy and more fortunate were drawn to works of charity. The Society of St. Vincent de Paul, founded in 1833 by Frederic Ozanam in Paris, is dedicated to the service of the poor in parishes and dioceses throughout the world. Vincent died in Paris on September 27, 1660, and was named patron of all Catholic charitable societies by Pope Leo XIII.

O God, be merciful to those in need.

ST. WENCESLAUS September 28
(907-929) martyr

ST. WENCESLAUS was born near Prague, Czechoslovakia, in 907. His father was Ratislav, Duke of Bohemia, and his mother was Drahomira, daughter of the chief of the Veletians. Wenceslaus was raised a Christian by his aunt, St. Ludmila. When he was a

222

young man, his father was killed while fighting the Magyars and his mother took over the government. She instituted secular or anti-Christian policies and angered Ludmila. She was murdered in 921 and replaced by Wenceslaus in 922.

Intent on molding his people in the faith he loved, Wenceslaus met fierce opposition from powerful elements among his own nobility after he became king. While in power, he cultivated friendly relations with Germany and in 926, he acknowledged King Henry I as the legitimate successor of Charlemagne.

When his brother, Boleslaus, lost the right of succession, he began to plot against Wenceslaus. He invited Wenceslaus to Stara Boleslav to celebrate the feast of Sts. Cosmas and Damian. Wenceslaus spent the evening and awoke the next morning to go to Mass. Along the way, he ran into Boleslaus, who with a group of companions, betrayed him and then murdered him on September 20, 929. St. Wenceslaus is the patron of Czechoslovakia.

Lord, give those who rule and govern
a spirit of wisdom and justice.

STS. MICHAEL, GABRIEL   September 29
and
RAPHAEL   archangels

HOLY SCRIPTURE speaks of angels as ministers of God in human affairs. St. Michael defends the honor of God against Satan. St. Gabriel announced to Mary the coming of Jesus. St. Raphael guided Tobias on his journey and brought healing to Tobit, his blind father.

As servants of God, the angels are instruments of God's hidden providence. They preserve us from harm, give God's wisdom and strength to humanity, and accompany us on our journey through life.

We thank you, Lord, with all our hearts;
in the presence of your angels we bless you.

ST. JEROME   September 30
(340-420) priest and doctor

ST. JEROME was born in 340 in Stridon, a small town in north Italy near today's Italian-Yugoslavian border. He was given an excellent classical education by his parents and was tutored by Donatus, the famous pagan grammarian, in Rome. As a result, Jerome became an expert in the Greek and Latin languages. In 360, at the age of eighteen, he was baptized in Rome by Pope Liberius. After his baptism, he traveled throughout the Roman Empire and was acquainted with many of the leading Christians of his day. He settled at Aquileia in 370 and became acquainted with St. Valerian.

Jerome went to Antioch in 374. In a dream, he saw himself in judgment before Christ, who rebuked him for his vain pursuit of worldly wisdom. Touched deeply by the dream, Jerome withdrew into the wilderness where, beset by temptations of many kinds, he "threw himself at the feet of Jesus, watering his feet with tears of prayers and penance," as he said later. To occupy himself, he began an intense study of Hebrew under a Jewish teacher. He found this study extremely difficult, but it prepared him for one of his great life works. He was ordained by St. Paulinus and went to Constantinople about 380 to study Scripture under St. Gregory Nazianzen. When Gregory left Constantinople, Jerome went to Rome in 382.

Pope Damasus asked him to be his secretary and in this capacity Jerome began his monumental translation of the Bible from Greek into Latin; it is called the Vulgate. "Not to know the Scriptures is not to know Christ," Jerome said. At the same time, his learned commentaries on the Scriptures and his conferences and letters won him a devoted following, especially among the Christian women of Rome.

Jerome, however, had his share of critics who resented his biting tongue and caustic comments on Roman society. Stung by their attacks on him, in

385 he left Rome for the Holy Land, where he established a number of communities near Bethlehem. There he not only continued his study of Scripture, but heatedly engaged in the controversies raging on the Church of his day. Jerome was sometimes ill-tempered and harsh in his dealings with others, yet he sought God's mercy again and again for himself and those he had injured.

When Alaric and his barbarians attacked Rome in 410, great numbers of Roman Christians fled to Palestine for safety. Jerome tried to arrange shelter for them and wrote, "I have put aside all my study to help them. Now we must translate the words of Scripture into deeds, and instead of speaking holy words we must do them." He died at Bethlehem of a long illness on September 30, 420. He is buried at St. Mary Major in Rome. St. Jerome is a Doctor of the Church.

Lord, show me your mercy
    and make my heart glad.
I am like the man going to Jericho
    wounded by robbers:
Good Samaritan, come help me.
    I am like the sheep gone astray:
Good Shepherd, come seek me
    and bring me home safe.
Let me dwell in your house all my days
    and praise you forever. Amen.

                                          St. Jerome

OCTOBER

ST. THÉRÈSE OF THE CHILD JESUS
(1873-1897) virgin

MARIE-FRANCOISE-THÉRÈSE MARTIN, born on January 2, 1873, at Alençon, France, was the youngest of nine children born to Louis and Azélie-Marie Martin. Her father was a successful watchmaker and her mother a seamstress. Her mother died when Thérèse was four years old and the child suffered a deep sadness and sense of loss that affected her for the next eight years of her life. After the death of her mother in 1877, Mr. Martin moved the family to Lisieux. In Lisieux, Thérèse was cared for by two older sisters, Mary and Pauline, and an aunt, Mrs. Guérin.

On Christmas Day, 1886, the young girl experienced a profound conversion. She developed a great love for the missionary life of the Church, her desire for prayer increased, and she began to make plans for entering the Carmelite convent in Lisieux, where her two older sisters, Mary and Pauline, were members.

By special dispensation she entered the Carmelites on April 9, 1888, and was professed on September 8, 1890. For the next seven years, she lived a life of prayer, fulfilling her routine duties with extraordinary faithfulness and love. She guided the novices of her community for the last four years of her life until she died on September 30, 1897, from a painful condition of tuberculosis.

After her death her spiritual autobiography, *The Story of a Soul*, revealed to the world her remarkable interior life of which even many of her own sisters in the convent were unaware.

Also known as "the Little Flower," Thérèse inspired millions of people by the spirit of her "little way." She became holy, Pope Pius XI said, "without going beyond the ordinary circumstances of life." Her love transformed everything she did, however small, into a pleasing gift for God.

Lord Jesus, I am not an eagle.
All I have are the eyes and the heart of one.
In spite of my littleness, I dare to gaze
    at the sun of love,
    and long to fly toward it.
I want to imitate the eagles,
    but all I can do is flap my small wings.
    What shall I do?

With cheerful confidence I shall stay
    gazing at the sun, till I die.
    Nothing will frighten me, neither wind nor rain.

O my beloved sun, I delight in feeling small
    and helpless in your presence;
    and my heart is at peace.

                                        St. Thérèse of the Child Jesus

"HE HAS given his angels charge over you, to keep you in all your ways" (Ps. 91).

Both the Old and New Testament recognize that God gives each person born into this world an angel guardian. Jesus, calling a little child to him, said that the angels in heaven watch over children such as this one. By a loving providence God reaches into human life to guard, protect and lead us on our way to salvation.

> *In the presence of the angels,*
> *I will sing to you, my God.*

ST. FRANCIS OF ASSISI   October 4
(1182-1226)

ST. FRANCIS was born at Assisi, Italy, in 1182. The son of a wealthy cloth merchant, he enjoyed the benefits of his father's success: good food, fine clothing and entertainment, a busy social life, and a place in his father's business. Love of adventure prompted him to become involved in the wars then waged through the cities and regions of Italy.

On his way to battle at Spoleto one day, when he was in his early twenties, he became ill and heard a voice telling him to "serve the master rather than men." Returning to Assisi, he experienced a great change within himself. Meeting a leper on the road, he embraced him and gave him alms. He began to visit the sick and support the poor. Praying one day before the crucifix in the deserted country church of St. Damian, he heard a voice saying to him, "Francis, go and rebuild my house; it is falling down." In 1206, the young man left and sold his goods to repair the poor churches in his neighborhood and to care for the needy.

His father, thinking his son had gone mad, summoned him before the bishops. Francis stripped off his clothes and giving them to his father said, "I have called you my father on earth, but now I say, 'Our Father, who art in heaven.'" He left his father's home to follow Christ as a poor man, vowing to keep the words of the Gospel literally. Francis wished to preach the kingdom of heaven, to give freely what he received, to possess neither gold nor silver.

Joyful, simple, a lover of people and nature, Francis soon attracted companions who shared his love of Christ and the Gospel. In 1210, he went to Rome to seek approval of his way of life from Pope Innocent III. Blessing his endeavor and officially recognizing the Franciscans, the pope afterwards told of a dream in which he saw Francis holding up the pillars of the Church. He was joined by St. Clare in 1212 and convened over five thousand Franciscans at Assisi in 1219 for the General Chapter of Mats.

With his call to return to the spirit of the Gospel, Francis gave new life to the Christian people of Italy and Europe. Missionaries were sent to Tunis and Morocco for the first time in 1219. He also traveled to the Holy Land where he preached to the Moslems and visited the places where Jesus lived and died. During this journey, he unsuccessfully tried to convert Sultan Malek al-Kamil of Egypt. His deep affection for the events of Jesus' life inspired him to recreate the Holy Child's birth at Christmas by erecting a creche at Grecchia in 1223. He loved the Passion of Jesus so much that he received the wounds of Christ known as the stigmata on his own body on the feast of the Holy Cross in 1224. "Nothing comforts me so much as to think of the life and Passion of our Lord," he said. "Were I to live till the end of the world I would need no other book."

In poor health and half blind, Francis died welcoming his Sister Death, while the Passion of Jesus was read aloud from the Gospel on October 3, 1226.

Praised be my Lord and God, with all his creatures,
and especially our brother the sun, who brings us
the day and brings us the light: fair is he,
and he shines with great splendor.

O Lord, he is a sign to us of you!

Praised be my Lord for our sister the moon,
and for the stars, set clear and lovely
in heaven. St. Francis

ST. BRUNO
(1035-1101) priest

ST. BRUNO was born at Cologne, Germany, in 1035. He was educated at the cathedral school of Rheims and returned to Cologne in 1055 and was ordained. He became a canon in the Collegiate Church of St. Cunibert and returned to Rheims in 1056 to teach theology. He was appointed chancellor of Rheims by Archbishop Manasses in 1074 and sought to reform the clergy and to end abuses of clerical power.

In 1082, Bruno decided to abandon ecclesiastical life and left Rheims with two companions. He lived a life of solitude and prayer under St. Robert, abbot of Molesmes, at Sèche-Fontaine. In 1084, he left for Grenoble with six companions. St. Hugh, Bishop of Grenoble, befriended the group and assigned to them the desert of Chartreuse for their settlement. An oratory was built, and Bruno founded the Carthusian Order, which is devoted to the hermit's way of life.

In 1090, Pope Urban II, whom Bruno had taught as a student, called his former teacher to Rome as his advisor. Bruno refused all ecclesiastical honors, including the bishopric of Reggio, and desired to remain alone with God. He retired to Calabria and founded two hermitages, St. Mary's and St. Stephen's. He died at Calabria on October 6, 1101.

Lord, you alone are God.
You alone are Lord.

OUR LADY OF THE ROSARY   October 7

THIS FEAST was established by St. Pius V to commemorate the victory of the Christian naval fleet, commanded by Don Juan of Austria, against the Turks at Lepanto on October 7, 1571. Don Juan attributed the great victory to the intercession of the Blessed Mother, which was invoked by the praying of the Rosary.

The Rosary was revealed to St. Dominic by the Blessed Mother about the beginning of the thirteenth century, and is one of the most beautiful of all devotions.

The Rosary, a summary of the Christian faith, has always enabled Christians to approach Jesus with Mary who "kept all these things in mind, treasuring them in her heart." As one recent pope has said, "The recitation of the Rosary helps the individual to meditate on the mysteries of the Lord's life as seen through the eyes of her who was closest to the Lord." (Pope Paul VI)

O God, by the life, death, and resurrection of your Son, Jesus Christ, you filled the world with joy. Grant, that meditating on the mysteries of the most holy Rosary of the Blessed Virgin Mary we may both imitate what they contain and obtain what they promise through Christ Our Lord.

ST. DENIS bishop and martyr October 9
and COMPANIONS (d. 258) martyrs

ACCORDING TO tradition, St. Denis was born in Italy. About the year 250, he went to France with six companions and became the first Bishop of Paris. Denis was arrested with two of his companions, Rusticus and Eleutherius, because of their efforts to convert the citizens of Rome to Christianity. They suffered martyrdom in 258 under the persecution of Decius. The Benedictine abbey of Denis was built over their burial site.

Legend says he was put to death at Montmartre, "the Martyr's Mount," in that city and after execution walked with his head under his arm to the present site of the abbey that bears his name. In art he is represented as a bishop holding his head in his hands. He is honored as the patron of Paris and of France.

Lord, you send disciples to all the nations,
send your truth to all peoples.

ST. JOHN LEONARDI October 9
(1541-1609) priest

ST. JOHN LEONARDI was born at Lucca, Italy, in 1541. During his early years the Council of Trent was completing the great reforms that would influence the future of the Catholic Church. He was ordained in 1572 and founded a community of priests to foster the work of catechetical instruction recommended by the Council. The community, formally recognized by Pope Clement VIII in 1595, is known as the Clerks Regular of the Mother of God. In 1579 he founded the Confraternity of Christian Doctrine, wrote a book on Christian doctrine, and sought to train the laity as teachers of religion.

At Rome he opened a seminary to train priests for missionary areas throughout the world. In 1603, his efforts led to the foundation of the College of the Propagation of the Faith, which has trained thousands of missionary priests over the last 300 years.

John is an example of one who heard the call of the Spirit to reform the Church and labored without end to build a holy Church. He died at Rome on October 9, 1609, a victim of the plague which had ravaged the city.

Lord, you will that all people be saved.
May the message of faith be
proclaimed everywhere.

ST. CALLISTUS I
(d. 222) pope and martyr

ACCORDING TO tradition, St. Callistus was a Roman slave and a Christian. As a slave, he was put in charge of a bank by Carpophorus, his master. Eventually, the bank failed and he fled from Rome. He was caught and sentenced to the hand mill. In time, Callistus was released by his creditors, but was rearrested and sentenced to labor in the mines of Sardinia. He was later released at the request of Marcia, a friend of the Emperor Commodus. In 199, Callistus was named director of a Christian cemetery in Rome on the Via Appia by Pope Zephyrinus. The cemetery still exists today and bears Callistus' name.

Freed from slavery, Callistus served the Church as deacon and succeeded Zephyrinus as Pope in 217. He upheld the Catholic belief in the Trinity against heretical teachers and the antipope, St. Hippolytus.

His forgiveness of repentant murderers and adulterers, and other acts of kindness toward those who had fallen into sin and showed human weakness caused his enemies to call him too lax and lenient. Callistus, however, knew the power of God's mercy and love. Like Jesus, he saw the Church as the Good Samaritan who came to bind up the wounds of the sinful people. He suffered martyrdom in 222 and was buried on the Aurelian Way.

Lord, you are rich in mercy, forgive us our sins.

ST. TERESA OF AVILA   October 15
(1515-1582) virgin and doctor

ST. TERESA was born at Avila, Spain, on March 28, 1515, the daughter of an influential family in that town. Lively and affectionate by nature, she made friends easily and adapted readily to any circumstance.

As a child she was drawn to religion. She and her small brother avidly read the lives of the saints and once even attempted to leave home to die for their faith among the Moors in Africa. They were quickly returned home.

Teresa's religious values weakened in her teenage years. In 1531, however, she suddenly decided to enter the Carmelite monastery at Avila over her father's objection. She was professed in 1538. After a period of sickness and religious mediocrity, she began to experience great graces of prayer in her late thirties. She described her experiences with remarkable skill in writings that have become spiritual classics. Her *Autobiography*, *The Way of Perfection*, and *The Interior Castle* have inspired and guided countless people in their spiritual lives.

Teresa decided to reform her own Carmelite community with the help of Sts. Peter of Alcantara and John of the Cross and she established new monasteries throughout Spain. Despite much opposition she went about her task with a good disposition and great common sense. She was both a mystic and a practical apostle.

As she lay dying, the Holy Eucharist was brought to her bedside. "O my Lord, now it is time that we may see each other," she exclaimed. She died at Alba de Tormes, Spain, on October 4, 1582, surrounded by her sisters who had been enriched so much by her wisdom and example. She is a Doctor of the Church.

Strenghten and prepare my soul, good Jesus,
*   and help me do something for you.*
For no one could possibly receive as much as I have
*   and give nothing in return.*
Whatever it takes, Lord, may I not come before you
*   with empty hands, since we are rewarded*
*   according to our deeds.*

Here is my life, my honor, my will;
*   I give all to you.*
*   Do with me what you will.*
I can do little, but approaching you
*   I can do all things,*
*   if you do not leave me.*

ST. HEDWIG   October 16
(1174-1243) religious

ST. HEDWIG was born at Andechs, Bavaria, in 1174. She was the daughter of Count Berthold IV of Andechs and married Duke Henry of Silesia in

1186 at the age of twelve. They would have seven children.

A woman of faith and love she provided care for the weak and the elderly, lepers and those in prison, travelers and the sick. Her generosity built hospitals and monasteries throughout her land, including the Cistercian monastery for nuns at Trebnitz. She intervened to make peace between her warring sons, Henry and Conrad, who were quarreling over land and power. With a mother's care she embraced the needs of all her people.

After her husband's death in 1238, she entered the monastery of Trebnitz and died there on October 15, 1243. Many miracles were attributed to her intercession.

> O God, giver of all gifts,
>   make us generous to those in need.

ST. MARGARET MARY ALACOQUE (1647-1690) virgin

October 16

ST. MARGARET MARY was born in the Burgundy region of France in 1647. As a young girl she suffered from a crippling rheumatic condition and, after her father's death in 1655, insensitive treatment from other members of her family. In 1671, she entered the Visitation convent at Paray-le-Monial. She was favored in prayer by special revelations which began on December 27, 1673, in which the Lord called her to reveal to the world the love of his Sacred Heart. These revelations would continue for nearly two years. Despite the misunderstanding of some of her sisters, Margaret Mary continued to speak of this mystery of Christ, doing everything the Lord required of her.

The Heart of Jesus, she wrote, "contains all blessings and into it the poor should cast all their needs. It contains all joy to take away all our sorrows. It contains all humility, to counteract our foolishness. It contains all mercy, all love to meet our every need."

With the help of Blessed Claude de la Colombiere, S.J., who declared that the revelations were genuine, Margaret Mary promoted the devotions of the nine First Fridays and the Holy Hour, and through her efforts the feast of the Sacred Heart was established in the Church. At a time when Christian fervor was growing cold, Margaret Mary recalled the great love that God has for his people.

She died at Paray-le-Monial on October 17, 1690. Her shrine is a favorite place of pilgrimage in France.

O Sacred Heart of Jesus, I put my trust in you.

ST. IGNATIUS OF ANTIOCH October 17
(d. 107) bishop and martyr

ST. IGNATIUS, the second Bishop of Antioch, Syria, was a convert and a disciple of St. John the Evangelist. He was appointed Bishop of Antioch about the year 69 by St. Peter. In 107, during the reign of Emperor Trajan, he was sentenced to death and brought under guard to Rome to be killed by wild beasts. On his way to Rome, he traveled through Asia Minor and Greece. Along the way he wrote seven letters to Christians in communities that contacted him on his final journey.

Thanking them for their concern, he told them to be faithful to the teaching they had received and begged them not to prevent his death for Christ. "I know what is to my advantage. At last I am becoming his disciple. May nothing entice me till I happily make my way to Jesus Christ! Fire, cross, struggles with wild beasts, wrenching of bones, mangling of limbs —let them come to me, provided only I make my way to Jesus Christ. I would rather die and come to Jesus Christ than be king over the entire earth. Him I seek who died for us; him I love who rose again because of us."

With a special sense that life does not end here on earth, Ignatius went bravely to his death. He knew he was following Jesus in his Passion and would rise in his Resurrection. As he wrote to the Romans, "Permit me to imitate my suffering God... I am God's wheat and I shall be ground by the teeth of beasts, that I may become the pure bread of Christ."

Ignatius urged the Christians of his day to be united in the faith they had received from the apostles. No false teaching should lead them astray. Jesus Christ was their Lord. They were to listen to their bishops. He died at Rome on December 20, 107, after being devoured by two lions in the amphitheatre.

Be deaf to anyone who does not speak of Jesus Christ.
He was descended from David,
  truly was he born of Mary.
He ate and drank,
  truly was he tried by Pontius Pilate.
He was crucified,
  truly he died, as heaven and earth looked on.
He was raised from the dead,
  truly his Father wakened him.
And his Father will raise us, too,
  who believe in him in Christ Jesus;
  truly we have no life except in Jesus Christ.

St. Ignatius, to the Trallians

ST. LUKE   October 18
   (first century) evangelist

BORN OF a pagan family, St. Luke became a convert to the Christian faith. He accompanied St.

Paul on his second missionary journey and was with the apostle during his final imprisonment in Rome. Paul calls him "my dear friend Luke" in one of his epistles.

Luke compiled the third Gospel. He describes at length the infancy of Jesus and emphasizes the Lord's prayerfulness and his mercy. The great parable of the Prodigal Son is found in Luke. The evangelist writes sensitively of Jesus' regard for women as well as his interest in the underprivileged and the outcasts of his society.

In the Acts of the Apostles Luke relates the beginnings of the infant Church as it develops under the inspiration of the Holy Spirit.

He saw clearly the continuity of the Church from the time of Jesus to its later expansion into the Gentile world. In his writings the Church's roots go back to the traditions of Israel and its future will touch all the nations of the earth. The Holy Spirit, descending at Pentecost, guides her with surprising wisdom and power, leading individuals and the Church herself to undertake new ventures despite human reluctance and fear.

One tradition says that Luke died at Boeotia, in Greece, at the age of eighty-four. He is patron of painters and physicians. In art he is represented by an ox because he begins his Gospel with the account of the priest Zachary sacrificing in the temple.

Lord Jesus, may we grow in faith
through the words of your Gospel.

ST. ISAAC JOGUES (d. 1647) October 19
and
ST. JOHN DE BRÉBEUF (d. 1649)
and COMPANIONS priests and martyrs

EIGHT MEMBERS of the Society of Jesus, six of them priests and two lay associates, were killed in North America by Indians from the Huron and Iroquois tribes between the years 1642 and 1649.

René Goupil, a doctor at an Indian mission near Quebec, was captured by the Iroquois in 1642 and killed after barbaric torture. Isaac Jogues, a priest, was also captured with Goupil but managed to escape to New York and returned to France after being severely mutilated. Pope Urban VIII gave him a dispensation to celebrate Mass with his mangled hands. "It cannot be that a martyr of Christ not drink the blood of Christ."

Returning to Canada in 1644, Jogues together with Jean de Lalande was captured by a Mohawk war party near Auriesville, New York. They were tomahawked on October 18, 1647 as they went about their missionary duties.

Anthony Daniel, a Jesuit priest, was killed after celebrating Mass at the mission of St. Joseph near Quebec. An Iroquois war party attacked the mission and shot him while he was ministering to the wounded on July 4, 1648.

Jean de Brébeuf and Gabriel Lalement were captured by the Iroquois near the town of St. Ig-

nace in Canada on March 16, 1649. Tied to stakes they were cruelly tortured for three hours before dying. In his diary de Brébeuf had written: "Jesus, what can I give for all the favors you have given me? I will take from your hand the cup of suffering and call on your name . . . I vow to you, Jesus my Savior, that as far as I have strength I will never fail to accept the grace of martyrdom, if some day you in your infinite mercy should offer it to me, your unworthy servant."

Charles Garnier and Noel Chabanel also suffered death in Canada at the hands of Indians. These brave missionaries were responsible for the first beginnings of the faith in North America. They were willing to endure any hardship to bring the word of the Gospel to a new continent.

O God, may our faith be so strong
that we should die for you.

ST. PAUL OF THE CROSS   October 19
(1694-1775) priest

ST. PAUL FRANCIS DANEO, founder of the Passionists, was born at Ovada, Italy, on January 3, 1694. He was the eldest of six children who survived from a family of fifteen. His merchant father, Luca, and his mother, Anna Maria, gave him their own deep faith and courage. Early in life Paul knew the meaning of life and death. Sensitive and enthusiastic, he was mostly self-taught, with an excellent memory and good appreciation of human nature.

In July 1713, while listening to a sermon preached by his parish priest, he received an interior grace that drew him closely to God. Influenced by this original fervor he went in 1715 to enroll in an armed crusade from Venice against Turkish invaders. He hoped to give his life for his faith. On his way to enlist, however, he stopped to visit the Blessed Sacrament in a church and saw clearly that his vocation was not to be a soldier, but that it was to take another form. From 1717 to 1720, he received many graces that indicated he was to found a community to keep alive the memory of the Passion of our Lord. Under the guidance of Bishop Di Gottinara he made a long retreat of forty days in which God prepared his spirit for his life work as a missionary and founder of a religious community.

After serving the sick at the hospital of San Gallicano in Rome, he was ordained a priest in 1727 by Pope Benedict XIII. With six companions he went to live on Monte Argentario and began a long career as a preacher and spiritual director. His sermons on the Passion of Jesus moved the hearts of many in the poor and neglected areas of central Italy. The most hardened of sinners were changed after hearing him speak. Great numbers of men and women were led to deep prayer and union with God through his guidance. He took upon himself the burdens of the people he met and often experienced great desolation and abandonment by God. Yet Paul continued with patient faith to preach and minister to the people at every opportunity.

For over fifty years, he preached the Passion of Christ by word and example. This "Hunter of Souls," as he was called, planted and revived the faith wherever he labored. He died at Rome on October 18, 1775, in his eighty-second year.

Communities of Passionist men and women, inspired with his dedication to Christ Crucified, are throughout the world today.

O God,
　　turn our minds and hearts
　　to the merciful Cross of your Son.

　　Help us to continue in faith and love
　　and assist us in every need.

ST. JOHN OF CAPISTRANO   October 23
(1386-1456) priest

ST. JOHN was born at Capistrano, Italy, of an influential family in 1386. He studied law at Perugia, began a career in government, and was appointed governor of Perugia in 1412. After he suffered reverses in his life he was converted to God, entered the Franciscans, and was ordained in 1420. A disciple of St. Bernardino of Siena, he accompanied the saint in his preaching ministry and was profoundly influenced by his holiness.

John undertook many missions for Church reform in behalf of the papacy. After the fall of Constantinople, he inspired the people of Hungary to defend their land against Turkish invaders. During the Battle of Belgrade in 1456, his courage lifted the spirits of the Christian army and helped them to victory.

John Capistrano, through his preaching, writing and involvement in the controversies of his time, won a place of leadership in his order and his Church. He died at Villach, Austria, on October 23, 1456.

O God, you renew the world through your saints.
  Give us saints for today.

ST. ANTHONY CLARET   October 24
  (1807-1870) bishop

ST. ANTHONY was born at Sallet, Spain, in 1807. A weaver's son, he worked in a textile mill in Barcelona and learned the printing trade. Ordained a priest in 1835, he entered the Jesuit novitiate at Rome, but returned to Spain in 1837 to devote himself to preaching missions and retreats throughout Catalonia. One of Spain's great preachers, he sometimes preached as many as twelve sermons in one day. A number of young priests joined him in his ministry. The community he founded in 1849 became known as the Claretians.

In 1845, he was appointed Archbishop of Santiago, Cuba, where he succeeded in bringing about reforms in the Church of that country even though his life was threatened. Queen Isabella II of Spain recalled him to be her advisor in 1857, and Anthony began a new phase of his ministry. He resigned his Cuban archbishopric in 1858, became influential in Spanish political life, and worked tirelessly to instruct the people in their faith. Besides his constant preaching he published over 200 books and pamphlets on religious subjects and established the Religious Publishing House, an influential Catholic publishing house, in Barcelona. In the revolution of 1868, Anthony was exiled with Queen Isabella II. He went to France, where he died near Narbonne on October 24, 1870.

Father, may your ways be known
upon earth.

ST. SIMON
and
ST. JUDE
(first century) apostles

LITTLE IS known of Sts. Simon and Jude except that they were chosen by Jesus as apostles and appear well down on the list of twelve. They do not figure prominently in the Gospel stories, as do some other apostles. After Jesus' Ascension there is no reliable account of what happened to them. Stories of their founding the Church in Syria and Egypt are groundless.

Unlike Sts. Peter and Paul, whose words and deeds are widely reported in Scripture and whose achievements dramatically affected the society of their day, Simon and Jude appear to have done little in their lives that was notable. Yet the Church celebrates them among her founders, seeing their preaching revealing God to us and their prayers aiding her growth.

The apostles were not all of one mold. Some, like Peter and Paul, were active public figures immersed in the controversy and changing movements of their time. Others, perhaps like Simon and Jude, may have taken a quieter path. Yet their voices too have been heard through all the earth.

Not only brilliant, active, and achieving apostles communicate the faith. Some, also apostles, may pass on this treasure in simpler, unnoticed ways; ordinary sowers, they cast the seed of faith undramatically on a world waiting for harvest.

Lord,
   may we follow and serve you.

NOVEMBER

THIS FEAST which has its beginnings in the Christian churches of the fifth and sixth centuries celebrates all those saints, canonized or not, who enjoy the happiness of the kingdom of heaven. Our relatives and friends, multitudes unknown "which no one can number from all tribes and peoples and tongues," stand before God's throne in joyful praise. They are remembered this day. God's amazing grace has brought them home.

And we are united to them. The ancient creeds proclaimed a communion of saints, a bond between the Church on earth and those in heaven, a sharing of love and grace. Because of that union the saints inspire those below to follow in their steps; their prayers rise up for us. They remind us of the joy that awaits us and our call to join them as children in our Father's house.

"Now that they are welcomed in their own country and at home with the Lord, through him, with him and in him, they intercede unceasingly with the Father in our behalf. Their care is the greatest help to our weakness." (Pope Paul VI)

The feast of All Saints turns our eyes to that "great cloud of witnesses" who are with God, yet still with us. We share in their love and are inspired by their example. They attract us to journey to the Kingdom of God.

For all the saints who from their labors rest,

Who thee by faith before the world confessed,
Thy name, O Jesus, be forever blest!
  Alleluia, alleluia!

ALL SOULS   November 2

THE EARLY Christians, like their pagan ancestors, remembered their dead on certain days of the year. The present date for our yearly commemoration of the dead was established in the tenth century. We remember the dead prayerfully so that God will "strengthen our hope that all our departed brothers and sisters will share in Christ's resurrection."

In the words of Vatican Council II, "Fully conscious of the Mystical Body of Jesus Christ, the Church on earth honors with great respect the memory of the dead, and, because it is a holy and wholesome thought to pray for the dead that they may be freed from their sins (2 Mac. 12, 46), she offers her suffrages for them."

Lord God, Maker of all,
Master of life and death,
Guard and gift of our souls,
receive those who go before us on the
    pilgrimage of death;
in due time receive us too when our days are done.

May we come,

not troubled by fear,
not clinging to this world,
not turning from your welcome,
but drawn to our life in heaven,
blessed and everlasting in Jesus Christ, our Lord.

St. Gregory Nazianzen

ST. MARTIN DE PORRES   November 3
(1579-1639) religious

ST. MARTIN was born at Lima, Peru, on November 9, 1579. He was the illegitimate son of a prominent Spanish colonist, John de Porres, and a poor black woman, Anna Velasquez. For some years his father refused to recognize him as his son, and so Martin shared his mother's poverty. After eight years, the father accepted Martin and provided for his education. With skills as pharmacist, doctor and surgeon, the youth began to work for the poor of his city. He asked to be admitted as a Dominican lay-helper at Rosary Convent in Lima. Eventually his community, impressed with his life of prayer and service, asked him to become a full member in 1594. He helped establish an orphanage and foundling hospital and spent much of his time caring for the black slaves brought to Peru from Africa.

Martin remained for the rest of his life a devoted servant of the poor, caring for their sick, treating them with dignity, reminding them of God's love for people of every race and color. Those who knew him called him a "loving father, a father of the poor." A close friend of St. Rose of Lima, Martin died at Rosary Convent in Lima on November 3, 1639.

> O God, you raise up those who are bowed down. Help the poor and distressed.

ST. CHARLES BORROMEO November 4 (1538-1584) bishop

ST CHARLES, the son of Count Gilbert Borromeo and Margaret Medici, sister of Pope Pius IV, was born into a noble and aristocratic family in the castle of Arona on Lake Maggiore, Italy, on October 2, 1538. He was educated at the Benedictine abbey of Sts. Gratinian and Felinus at Arona. He studied Latin at Milan and then attended the University of Pavia. He received his doctorate in 1559. In 1560, at the age of twenty-three, his uncle, Pope Pius IV, appointed him Secretary of State and Cardinal Deacon of Milan, entrusting him with many responsible positions in the service of the Church. Largely through Charles' efforts, the Council of Trent finished its work of Church reform in 1562.

Ordained a priest in 1563 and appointed Bishop of Milan shortly afterwards, Charles began a life-long labor to reform the ancient Christian city where he had been appointed bishop. Like his predecessor, St. Ambrose, he fostered the education of clergy, established the Confraternity of Christian Doctrine for the religious education of children, and cared for the poor. He himself lived a simple, sparing life, without concern for his own comfort. Though he suffered from a speech defect, he constantly preached to his people who received his words as if from a messenger of God.

When plague struck the area of Milan in 1576, Charles mobilized all the resources at his disposal to minister to the sick and the dying. He cared for the plague-stricken with his own hands and comforted them in their anguish until the plague subsided in 1578.

Other parts of the Church received his attention as well. The English college at Douai, France, which prepared priests for that troubled country, was founded through his efforts. He visited the neighboring country Switzerland in 1583 to support the Catholic faith there.

During his ministry as bishop, Charles had enemies among the civil administration and his own clergy. In 1569, while he knelt at prayer in church, an assassin, Jerome Donati Farina, a Humiliati priest, tried to murder him, but the bullet fell harmlessly from the cloak on his back.

On the evening of November 4, 1584, at the age of 46, he died in Milan after making his annual retreat at Monte Varallo.

O God, make us servants of your Gospel.

DEDICATION OF THE CHURCH OF ST. JOHN LATERAN

THE EMPEROR CONSTANTINE, after ending three centuries of Church persecution, gave the Lateran Palace in Rome for use as a church in 324. The church was named for St. John the Baptist and St. John the Evangelist. An early inscription describes this church as "the mother and head of all churches," because here the Christians of Rome were baptized. The Popes resided next to this church until the fourteenth century when they moved their residence to the Vatican.

The Catholic Church has always revered its churches as places of God's grace. Its people, "living stones," "temples of God," gather for worship there. God's word is proclaimed, his sacraments are celebrated within the church walls. As we celebrate the dedication of certain churches, we recall the holiness of every church as a house of prayer where God's love is at work preparing a family for the heavenly city of Jerusalem.

O God, we praise you in your temple.

ST. LEO THE GREAT   November 10
(d. 461) pope and doctor

NOTHING IS known of St. Leo's early life. He was probably born in Rome of Tuscan parents and served as deacon under St. Celestine I and Sixtus III. He was consecrated as Pope and elevated to the chair of St. Peter on September 29, 440. This was a time when savage barbarian tribes ravaged the Italian peninsula with repeated attacks. As the Roman civil administration began to disintegrate, the populace increasingly turned to the pope for leadership.

When Attila the Hun led his warriors into Italy in 452, Leo, accompanied by the civil leaders of Rome, went to meet him to plead for the city's safety. He was able to negotiate the barbarians' withdrawal by promising them annual tribute. Three years later, the Vandal warriors of Genseric appeared before the gates of Rome. This time Leo could not stop them from burning and looting the city, taking many captives with them to Africa for ransom. Leo directed the repair of the city and sent priests to minister to the captives in Africa.

Truly a rock like St. Peter, Leo preached eloquently to the people and strengthened their faith. He was staunchly opposed to Manichaeanism, Pelagianism, Priscillianism, and Nestorianism. He recognized his role to care for all the churches of Christendom and affirmed the primacy of the Bishop of Rome over the other bishops of the Church.

When some questioned whether Jesus was both God and man, Leo wrote a statement upholding the belief which was read to 600 bishops at the Council of Chalcedon in 451. "Peter has spoken through Leo!," the bishops cried in approval.

Leo died at Rome on November 10, 461.

Father,
    you will never allow the power
    of hell to prevail against your Church.

ST. MARTIN OF TOURS   November 11
(316-397) bishop

ST. MARTIN was born at Sabaria, Hungary, in 316. His father was a pagan soldier and moved the family to Pavia, Italy. Martin entered the Roman army at the age of fifteen and served as a soldier for twenty years. In 337, he was stationed at Amiens and had a vision of Christ in his sleep. He then left the army, converted to Christianity, and became a monk at a monastery near Poitiers, France. St. Hilary, who was the Bishop of Poitiers, received Martin as one of his disciples.

In Poitiers he became a soldier of another kind. The heresy of Arianism with its strong political backing seemed ready to crush the Catholic Church. Martin fought the Arians with words of true faith. Poverty and sickness oppressed many people in his region and Martin reached out to alleviate their need. Because of their opposition to Arianism, Hilary was exiled by Emperor Constantius and Martin by Auxentius, the Arian bishop. They both returned from exile to Poitiers in 360. Martin established the first monastic community in France at Ligugé. Despite his protests, Martin was elected Bishop of Tours in 371.

Martin always preferred a simple chair to his bishop's throne. He ate simple food and hardly thought of anything as his own. Once when he saw a shorn sheep he said: "This sheep teaches a lesson from the Gospel. She gave one of her coats to some-one who had none." From the many stories that tell of Martin giving away his own clothing to the poor, he kept that lesson well himself.

He retired from Tours and lived at the famous monastery at Marmoutier. The bishop never re-laxed his efforts to serve his people. Old and feeble, he visited throughout his diocese to reconcile quar-reling priests. In 384, St. Ambrose and Martin op-posed Ithacius, Bishop of Ossanova. He wanted the heretic, Priscillian, put to death, but they would not hear of it. Eventually Emperor Maximus had Pris-cillian put to death. In order to prevent further bloodshed, Martin reached a compromise with Ithacius, but was troubled by his decision.

While in a remote part of his diocese, Martin be-came very ill. When someone at his bed suggested that he turn on his side to relieve his discomfort he responded, "Let me look towards heaven rather

than earth so that my soul may journey on the right
course to the Lord."

Martin died on November 8, 397. France honors
him as one of her patrons.

> O God,
>> you called the peacemaker blessed.
>> Grant us the grace to struggle for peace
>> in our world.

ST. JOSAPHAT   November 12
(1580-1623) bishop and martyr

JOHN KUNSEVICH was born at Vladimir, Volhynia,
Poland in 1580. John became a merchant, but was
unhappy. In 1604, he entered the monastery of the
Holy Trinity at Vilna and became a monk. He took
the name of Josaphat and was ordained in 1609. He
began to work diligently for the reunion of the Orthodox Church with the Church of Rome.

In 1617, Josaphat became Bishop of Vitebsk,
Russia. Soon after, he was appointed Bishop of
Polotsk and sought to reform his vast diocese,
which was split by political and religious tensions.
His efforts were successful and by 1620 the diocese
was largely Catholic.

However, tensions still persisted. Archbishop
Meletius Smotritsky established an Orthodox
bishopric in Polotsk to rival the Catholic bishopric

of Josaphat. Though Josaphat was recognized as the legitimate Archbishop of Polotsk, there was much confusion. Leo Sapieha, the chancellor of Lithuania and also a Catholic, falsely declared that Josaphat was responsible for the state of unrest which existed in the country.

Josaphat decided to address the issue with courage and went to Vitebsk, which was a center of dissent. While preaching there, he was surrounded by an armed mob who killed him and cast his body into the Divina River. He died on November 12, 1623, and is honored as an apostle of the reunion of the Christian Churches.

Lord Jesus, may all your people be one.

ST. FRANCES XAVIER CABRINI   November 13 (1850-1917) virgin

ST. FRANCES XAVIER CABRINI, the youngest of thirteen children, was born at Sant Angelo Lodigiano, Italy, on July 15, 1850, and christened Maria Francesca. As a child she loved to hear stories about Christian missionaries in the far away lands of the Orient. She lost her parents in 1870. After first studying to be a teacher, she applied for membership in the missionary orders, but was refused because of her health. In 1874, Monsignor Serrati asked Frances to run the House of Providence Orphanage at Codogno. In 1877, she began a religious community with seven associates working with her at the House of Providence, known as the Missionary Sisters of the Sacred Heart. The congregation was approved by the Bishop of Lodi in 1880 and officially recognized by Rome in 1887. When she spoke to Pope Leo XIII about her dream to go as a missionary to China, he answered, "Not to the East but to the West." Frances heeded the request of Bishop Scalabrini of Piacenza that she work with Italian immigrants in the United States. Archbishop Corrigan of New York sent a formal invitation requesting her help.

In 1889, Frances went to New York and turned to North and South America to assist the millions of Catholic immigrants. In New York, Chicago, and the cities of South America she founded schools, orphanages, and hospitals. In thirty-five years she had crossed the sea thirty times and established sixty-seven houses of her order, The Missionary Sisters of the Sacred Heart. She once wrote, "I admit my weakness, I am afraid of the sea. If I had no holy motive I would have no courage to travel." She died of malaria at Columbus Hospital in Chicago, Illinois, on December 22, 1917, while preparing Christmas presents for hundreds of children. She was canonized by Pope Pius XII in 1946, the first American citizen to be so honored.

O God, give us strength to do all we can for you.

ST. ALBERT THE GREAT   November 15
(1206-1280) bishop and doctor

ST. ALBERT was born in the castle of Lauingen at Swabia, Germany, in 1206. His family was noble and aristocratic, and his father was the Count of Bollstädt. Against his family's wishes, he entered the Dominican Order in 1223. He received his doctorate from the University of Paris in 1245, and was named regent of the studia generalia at Cologne in 1248. He was one of the great teachers of his time and was an authority on physics, geometry, biology, geography, astronomy and the theological sciences. He taught at Cologne and Paris and had St. Thomas Aquinas, one of his closest associates, as a student. Those who knew him were amazed at his encyclopedic knowledge and his simple faith. They wondered how one person could know so much. Albert's study enabled succeeding generations of Christians to combine wide scholarly inquiry with Christian belief. Known as the "Universal Doctor," some of his great writings are *Summa Theologiae* and *Summa de Creaturis*.

In 1254, Albert was appointed provincial of the Dominicans in Germany. In 1260, he was named Bishop of Regensburg in Germany by Pope Urban IV who hoped Albert would bring reform to that diocese. Discovering that his talents were not in administration, Albert resigned his bishopric and returned to his teaching at Cologne after two years. He would then hold important positions in the papal court and in his order. He assisted at the Council of Lyons in 1274 and defended the teachings of St. Thomas Aquinas at the University of Paris against those who accused the great theologian of heresy.

In 1278, during a lecture his memory failed him. In the last two years of his life he was gradually deprived of his memory and his mind. He died quietly at Cologne, Germany, on November 15, 1280. He is the patron of those who study the natural sciences. Albert is a Doctor of the Church.

Lord, bless our minds with thoughts of you. Give us a love of truth.

ST. MARGARET OF SCOTLAND (1046-1093)

November 16

ST. MARGARET, the beautiful and talented daughter of Prince Edward d'Outremer (the Exile) and Princess Agatha of Hungary, was probably born in Hungary in 1046. The family went to England, but was forced to leave after William the Conqueror's victory at the Battle of Hastings in 1066. They were given refuge at the court of King Malcom III of Scotland. In 1070, at the age of twenty-four, Margaret married King Malcom III at the castle of Dunfermline. They had six sons and two daughters.

Margaret had a wonderful influence on her husband, calming his temper, inspiring him with good thoughts. Because of her example, the King became a model ruler.

In the same way, Margaret left her mark on her new country. She fostered religion and education among her people and promoted culture and works of charity. A number of churches were built through her interest.

She formed her own children to share in her strong faith. As future kings and queens, they showed their mother's spirit of prayer and concern for the poor.

In 1093, King William Rufus invaded Scotland and attacked Alnwick Castle. As Margaret lay ill and dying in Edinburgh Castle, her husband, King Malcom, and her son, Edward, were killed in battle. Four days later, Margaret died on November 16, 1093.

O God, give those who govern and rule
goodness and kindness of heart.

ST. GERTRUDE   November 16
(1256-1301) virgin

ST. GERTRUDE was born at Eisleben, Germany, in 1256. Nothing is known of her parents, and at the age of five she was put under the auspices of the

Benedictine nuns at Helfta. Intelligent and studious, she quickly mastered languages, literature, and philosophy in her early years. She would also enter the Benedictine Order at Helfta and become a nun.

At the age of twenty-six, she experienced the first of a series of revelations of Christ. In the chapel, "where I was accustomed to make my lukewarm prayers, I heard these words: 'I will save you and deliver you. Do not be afraid.'" From then on, she had numerous revelations and experiences of God's grace, which she wrote about in the *Book of Extraordinary Grace*, an account of her spiritual journey. As she approached death, she wrote, "I am certain whether my death be sudden or foreseen, that I shall never be without the mercy of God." Gertrude died at Helfta on November 17, 1301.

May my soul bless you, O Lord God my Creator, may my soul bless you. From my very being may all your merciful gifts sing your praise. Your care has been rich in mercy. Yes, it is without measure, and as far as I am able I give you thanks.   St. Gertrude

ST. ELIZABETH OF HUNGARY   (1207-1231)   November 17

ST. ELIZABETH, the daughter of King Andrew II of Hungary and Gertrude of Andechs-Meran, was

273

born at Pressburg, Hungary, in 1207. In 1221, at the age of fourteen, she married Louis of Thuringia. They loved each other deeply and Elizabeth gave birth to three children.

The young noblewoman was devoted to the poor and the sick. Because their castle was built high on a steep hill, Elizabeth constructed a hospital at the base of the hill and there tended the needy who came for her care. Her deep faith saw Christ in those who seemed most abandoned. One day before a crucifix in church, one biographer relates, she fell to her knees and cast her royal crown to the ground. When her husband asked what she was doing, she replied, "I cannot stand before the image of Christ with a crown of gold and pearls on my head." On one occasion when all her hospital beds were filled, she placed a tired leper in her own to give him some sleep.

In 1227, after six happy years of marriage, Louis died on his way to a Crusade with Emperor Frederick II, and his political enemies drove Elizabeth into exile. Unconcerned for her own power and possessions, she continued her works of charity, building a hospital for the sick in Marburg and begging for support of the poor. In 1228, she put aside her expensive clothes and jewels and dressed in the simple habit of a Franciscan Tertiary. Like the widow who fed Elijah from the last of her resources, she gave all she had to those in need in the name of Christ. She died at Marburg on November 17, 1231, at the age of twenty-four.

St. Elizabeth is the patroness of Catholic Charities and Franciscan Tertiaries.

> *O God, give us generous hearts*
> *to come when others are in need.*

DEDICATION OF THE CHURCHES OF STS. PETER AND PAUL apostles

THE TWO great apostles, Sts. Peter and Paul, are honored today in the ancient churches where their bodies are buried. The Basilica of St. Paul and the Vatican Basilica of St. Peter were built originally in the fourth century and are reminders of the apostles who founded the Roman Church and are still its protectors.

The early Christians marked the place where their founding apostles were martyred with special care. Peter, ancient sources report, was martyred on the Vatican hill in 64 near the obelisk not far from the circus of Caligula and Emperor Nero. He was buried nearby in a cemetery. The Emperor Constantine erected the first basilica of St. Peter over the burial site in 326 while Sylvester was Pope. Later in 1626, the present basilica designed during the Renaissance was built. Recent excavations have uncovered the ancient burial place of Peter under the papal altar of this church.

Paul, according to tradition, was beheaded along the Ostian Way in 67. Constantine built a large basilica there over his grave in 386. It was rebuilt after a fire in 1823 according to its former measurements. The apostle's grave is behind the basilica's triumphal arch.

> Lord, the company of your apostles
> praises you.

PRESENTATION
OF MARY

THIS FEAST celebrates the dedication of the church of St. Mary built in Jerusalem near the site of the Temple. According to an early tradition, probably legendary, Mary was born to Sts. Ann and Joachim in Jerusalem, in a neighborhood close by the temple. At twelve, she was presented there to learn the law of God. The present Church of St. Ann, a favorite place of pilgrimage, marks the ancient site today.

The Scriptures which spoke of the "Daughter of Sion" singing and rejoicing in the presence of the Lord (Zech. 2, 14-17) probably suggested to ancient Christian piety eager to know the details of Mary's life that the virgin was born in the city of Sion, Jerusalem. The apocryphal Gospel of James reported the details of Mary's early life which were portrayed in art by many great medieval artists.

*Mary, Mother of God, you are the temple of the Lord
and dwelling place of the Holy Spirit.*
Help us to please God.

ST. CECILIA
virgin and martyr

November 22

ST. CECILIA, according to Roman legend, was a young patrician woman of Rome who was a Christian. She was filled with love for God to whom she vowed her life and virginity. Forced into marriage by her father, she sang to God on her wedding day, praying for help. Soon after, Valerian, her husband, and Tiburtius, his brother, were miraculously converted to Christianity by a vision and gave themselves to the care of the sick and the burial of the dead.

They were martyred at Pagus Triopus, outside of Rome, along with a Roman official, Maximus, because they refused to sacrifice to the gods. Cecilia buried their bodies, and was herself brought to trial for her beliefs. So persuasive was she that her accusers converted to Christianity. Finally, the prefect, Almachius, sentenced her to be suffocated in the heated bath of her home. Despite the intense heat she was unharmed, so a soldier was sent to behead her. She was struck on the neck three times and lingered for three days before dying. A tomb marking her grave is found in the cemetery of St. Callistus in Rome. St. Cecilia is the patron of musicians.

> Listen, my daughter, hear my words:
> forget your own people and your father's house.
> The king desires your beauty:
> He is your lord, give honor to him. Ps. 44

ST. CLEMENT I November 23
(d. 100) pope and martyr

ST. CLEMENT was the third successor of St. Peter as the Bishop of Rome, and succeeded Pope Cletus in 91. Little is known of his life except that he knew Sts. Peter and Paul. He was exiled to the Crimea by Emperor Trajan, condemned to death and martyred for his faith about the year 100. Representing the Church of Rome, Clement wrote a famous letter to the Corinthians concerning the schism that had arisen in Corinth. In the letter, he urged the Corinthians to unity and peace.

> We pray. Lord, that you be our helper
>   and protector.
> Deliver those of us in distress;
>   raise up the fallen,
>   turn your face to the needy,

heal the sick,
bring back the erring,
feed the hungry,
ransom our prisoners,
help the weak to their feet,
comfort the faint-hearted.
Let all nations know you are God alone,
and Jesus Christ is your Son.
Show them that we too are your people
and the sheep of your flock.

Epistle to the Corinthians

ST. COLUMBAN   November 23
(d. 615) abbot

ST. COLUMBAN was born at West Leinster, Ireland,
at about the time of St. Benedict's death. He became on of the great leaders of Irish monasticism.
In 585, he set out for France with twelve companions and established numerous monasteries in
France, Germany, Switzerland, and Italy. Columban based his rule on the love of God and neighbor.
He prescribed a strict discipline of prayer, study
and work. With simple honesty and boldness, Columban confronted the powerful rulers of Europe
when he judged them acting against the Gospel.
Exiled to Italy, he founded the famous monastery
at Bobbio, where he died on November 23, 615.

Columban's rule, base on Irish monastic teaching, instructs the monk to have a good conscience, to be tenderhearted, to work hard, serve the sick, deal kindly with sinners, be simple in dress, be wise, learned, generous and courteous. His monasteries, like other monasteries throughout Europe, served as hospitals, hotels, model farms, and places of learning. At a time when civilization was threatened, the monastic movement provided islands of safety and culture. Columban's influence remained strong in monastic circles until Charlemagne ordered that The Rule of St. Benedict be followed in all the monasteries of his empire.

> Alone with none but thee, my God,
> I journey on my way:
> What need I fear, when thou art near,
> O King of night and day?
> More safe I am within thy hand
> than if a host did round me stand.
>
> St. Columban

ST. ANDREW   November 30
(first century) apostle

ST. ANDREW came from Bethsaida, a town in Galilee on the Lake of Genesareth. He became a disciple of St. John the Baptist, who sent him to see Jesus. After visiting the Lord, Andrew called his brother, Simon Peter, to come and meet the Messiah. Later, as Jesus was walking along the Sea of Galilee, he saw Peter and Andrew casting their nets into the sea. Jesus said, "Follow me and I will make you fishers of men."

Andrew accompanied Jesus throughout his public ministry, and his name appears in the story of the feeding of five thousand in the desert. After the death of Christ, he labored as a missionary in Scythia, Greece, and Turkey and established the Church at Constantinople. He was crucified on an X-shaped cross at Patras, Acaia. St. Andrew is the patron saint of Russia and Scotland.

*I bow before the Cross made precious by Christ,
my Master.
I embrace it as his disciple.*

St. Andrew

DECEMBER

ST. FRANCIS XAVIER December 3
(1506-1552) priest

ONE OF the greatest missionaries of the Church, St. Francis Xavier was born near Pamplona, Spain, at the castle of Xavier, on April 7, 1506. He entered the University of Paris in 1524 and received his degree of licentiate from the College of St. Barbara in 1528. While at St. Barbara, Francis befriended St. Ignatius Loyola, the founder of the Jesuits. He was among the first companions of Ignatius and was present with six others who took their vows in 1534 at Montmartre. Francis, along with Ignatius and four Jesuit companions, was ordained at Venice in 1537. In 1540, Ignatius Loyola appointed him to accompany Fr. Simon Rodriguez as the first Jesuit missionaries to the East Indies, then a Portuguese colony.

Appointed apostolic nuncio to the East, Francis left for India in 1541. After a long voyage and much hardship, he arrived at Goa on May 6, 1542. For eleven years, Francis labored along the coast of India and in Japan. During his travels he would visit Cape Comorin, Malacca, the Moluccas, near New Guinea, and Montai, near the Philippines.

In village after village he preached the Gospel, struggling to learn the native languages and living simply on the food available to him. Along the Indian coast he baptized and instructed great numbers of native Christians who had been ill-treated by the European colonists.

On August 15, 1549, Francis entered Japan. With the aid of some Japanese converts he had a translation made of Christian teaching, and in halting Japanese he recited it to all who would listen. A small nucleus of Christians was converted and these became the faithful foundation of the Church in Japan. Francis returned to India in 1551 and was appointed the first Jesuit provincial of the East and India.

Longing to bring the Gospel to China, a land then forbidden to foreigners, Francis made his way to Sancian, a small island near Hong Kong, but before he could embark on his new venture, he took ill and died on December 3, 1552.

Francis found enormous joy in his missionary life. As he wrote in a letter, "Here in this vineyard we cry to God: Lord, give me not so much joy in this life."

St. Francis Xavier is the patron of foreign missions.

> God of all peoples
> be mindful of those without belief.
> Created in your image, they do not
> know you or your Son Jesus Christ,
> their Savior who died for them.
>
> By the prayers and labors of your Church,
> free them from ignorance and unbelief
> and lead them to worship you.
>
> St. Francis Xavier

ST. JOHN DAMASCENE   December 4
(674-749) priest and doctor

ST. JOHN DAMASCENE was born at Damascus, Syria, about 674. He was the son of Mansur, a treasury official of Damascus, and was tutored by the monk Cosmas. When the Christians lost control of Damascus to Moslem invaders, his father continued to serve the new Moslem government of Caliph Yazid. It is thought that John succeeded his father in the post of chief revenue officer to Caliph Abdul Malek. As Moslem rule increasingly restricted the religious rights of Christians, John withdrew to the monastery of St. Sabas, near Jerusalem, about 715 and became a monk and priest.

In 726 the Byzantine Emperor, Leo the Isaurian, condemned the use of religious images by Christians. John spoke out for many of the bishops of the East against the interference of the secular government in religious matters. He gained the enmity of the Emperor and his successor, Constantine Copronymus, for his stand. Because Jesus Christ became flesh and lived, taught and died in human form, John wrote, the Christian faith supports the practice of representing the Lord, his mother, and the saints in pictures. Besides his defense of images, John wrote against other Christian heresies troubling the Church of this time.

Among John's extensive writings are the *Fount of Wisdom*, his synthesis of Greek theology, *Exposition of the Orthodox Faith, The Discourses Against the Attackers of Holy Images*, and a number of beautiful homilies honoring Mary, the Mother of God. A brilliant theologian, poet, eloquent writer and speaker, he is the last great theological figure of the early Greek Church.

He died on December 4, 749, and his room is still preserved at his monastery near Jerusalem. St. John Damascene is a Doctor of the Church.

> *O God, you nourished me with spiritual milk,*
> *the milk of your sacred words.*
>
> *You strengthened me with the body*
> *of our Lord Jesus Christ.*
>
> *O Jesus Christ, you humbled yourself*
> *to bear on your shoulders the straying sheep that*
> *was I, and feed me in verdant pastures,*
> *and nourish me with true teaching, so that I,*
> *in turn, could feed your flock.*
>
> St. John Damascene

ST. NICHOLAS   December 6
(fourth century) bishop

ST. NICHOLAS was born into a wealthy family at Patara, Lycia, Asia Minor. He was imprisoned during the persecution of Diocletian, attended the Council of Nicaea, and died at Myra, where he was buried in the cathedral. Nicholas was chosen Bishop of Myra and devoted himself to helping the poor.

Tradition says that Nicholas devoted himself to works of charity. Hearing that an impoverished father had to sell his three daughters into prostitution because he had no money for their marriage dowry, Nicholas threw a small bag of gold into the poor man's window on three different evenings, and his daughters were able to marry. Finally, he was discovered as the bearer of these gifts.

At one time, he saved three innocent young men from execution by the powerful civil governor, Eustathius. At another time he came to the aid of seamen who called for his help during a storm at sea off the coast of Lycia. Suddenly appearing on their ship, he manned the ropes and sails beside the weary sailors and brought the vessel to port. Another tale relates that during a famine in his country, Nicholas was able through his prayers to guide some passing ships filled with grain to come to relieve his starving people.

Needless to say, with stories like these to his credit, Nicholas became a popular saint after his death. Seamen throughout Europe and Asia, as well as his own people, adopted him as their patron. His relics were carried to Bari, Italy, in 1087, after the Moslem invasion of Asia Minor. Countless churches in England, France and Germany bear his name. In Germany he became associated with Christmas, and as a giver of gifts on that holy day he is known in America as the kind and generous "Santa Claus."

Lord,
> *giver of good gifts, make us generous to others,*
> *especially to the needy.*

ST. AMBROSE
December 7
(340-397) bishop and doctor

ST. AMBROSE, the son of a high Roman official, was born at Trier, Germany, in 340. After the death of his father, the family moved to Rome. Ambrose studied Greek, law and rhetoric and came under the tutelage of Anicius Probus, the praetorian prefect of Italy, who appointed him as his assessor. His ability was recognized by Emperor Valentinian, who appointed him Governor of Liguria and Aemilia, in 372.

Auxentius, the Arian Bishop of Milan, died in 374. A new bishop had to be elected, and the Milanese Christians were divided into quarreling factions. In order to bring peace to the election, Ambrose went to the church to address the people. While he was speaking, someone cried out, "Ambrose, bishop!". The people enthusiastically took up the cry. Ambrose was not even baptized at the time. Over his objections and at the insistence of Emperor Valentinian, Ambrose prepared for baptism and his consecration as bishop. He was baptized and consecrated Bishop of Milan on December 7, 374. He was about thirty-five years old.

Ambrose proved to be a great bishop and served his people unselfishly. No one came to see him without being graciously received. His sermons and his celebrations of the liturgy filled his people with inspiration. St. Augustine, converted and baptized by Ambrose in 387, tells of leaving the church moved within his heart by Ambrose's words and personality.

The city of Milan was then an important political center of the Roman Empire. Ambrose, always a loyal Roman, was also a strong defender of the rights of the Church against Arianism. He was often a mediator between rival political groups in the imperial court. When Emperor Valentinian began to meddle in the affairs of the Church, Ambrose proclaimed, "The Emperor is in the Church, not over it."

Ambrose was an advisor to Emperor Gratian and convinced him to forbid Arianism in the West, in 379. When Maximus killed Gratian in battle in 383, Ambrose was able to keep him out of Italy and confine himself to France, Spain and England. Despite their agreement, Maximus made plans to invade Italy in 387. After the invasion, the Eastern Emperor, Theodosius, was persuaded to come to the aid of Italy. Theodosius defeated Maximus and executed him in Pannonia. Valentinian II returned to Italy and Theodosius became ruler of both the Eastern and Western empires. At the urging of Ambrose, Theodosius publicly opposed Arianism within the Empire. After the murder of Valentinian II in 393, Theodosius, again at the insistence of Ambrose, abolished paganism in the Empire.

Though Theodosius respected Ambrose, there were problems between them. In 390, Theodosius, angered by the murder of Butheric, the governor, massacred thousands of people in Thessalonica. Ambrose condemned him and called him to do public penance before he would administer the sacraments to him. Theodosius acquiesced. He died in 393 in the arms of Ambrose.

Courageous and holy, a bishop who upheld God's truth and the good of his people and his nation, Ambrose died at Milan on Good Friday, April 4, 397. St. Ambrose is a Doctor of the Church.

Lord,
> *teach me to seek you,*
> *and reveal yourself to me as I seek.*

> *For I cannot seek you unless first you teach me,*
> *nor find you unless first you reveal yourself to me.*
St. Ambrose

THE IMMACULATE CONCEPTION OF MARY   December 8

THE SOLEMN feast of Mary's Immaculate Conception, celebrated nine months before the feast of her birth (September 8), recalls the Christian belief that Mary was preserved free from all stain of original sin from the moment of her conception by her mother, Ann. Because of her unique role as the mother of Jesus Christ, God endowed her with special graces and gifts. Like a new Eve, she brought new life to the world through her Divine Son.

The feast is also a reminder that the whole Church shares in Mary's privileges in some way. For this reason the feastday prayer asks God to "trace in our actions the lines of her love, in our hearts her readiness of faith."

The bishops of the United States, with firm belief in Mary's intercession, confided their new nation to her care under the title of her Immaculate Conception.

Mary immaculate, star of the morning,
chosen before the creation began,
chosen to bring, for thy bridal adorning,
woe to the serpent and rescue to man.

Bend from thy throne at the voice of our crying,
Bend to this earth which thy footsteps have trod;
Stretch out thine arms to us, living and dying,
Mary immaculate, Mother of God.

F. W. Weatherell

ST. DAMASUS I
(305-384) pope

ST. DAMASUS was born at Rome, in 305. He was named a deacon of the church where his father, who was a priest, served. Pope Liberius died in 366, and Damasus was elected Pope at the age of sixty-two. Ursinus, the antipope, was also elected by opponents of Damasus, but was exiled by Emperor Valentinian. During his long reign of almost eighteen years, he had to struggle with opposing factions and teachers of false doctrine in the city as well as in other parts of the Church. He promoted the position of the papacy and reverently preserved the spiritual heritage of preceded Christian generations. In 380, Emperors Theodosius in the East and Gratian in the West proclaimed Christianity to be the religion of the Roman Empire.

Damasus is the first Pope to refer to the Roman Church as the Apostolic See, a site where an apostle's authority rests. "It is not by decisions of councils that the Roman Church has been placed above other churches, but it has obtained the primacy by the words of our Savior, 'You are Peter and on this rock I build my Church.' The first see of the apostle Peter is the Roman Church." (Decretun gelasianum)

Appreciative of learning, Damasus appointed St. Jerome his secretary and commissioned him to make a more accurate translation of the Scriptures from the best available Greek manuscripts. The results were St. Jerome's biblical commentaries and his translation of the Bible, the Vulgate. During his papacy, the language of the liturgy was changed from Greek to Latin at Rome.

The Pope discovered and restored the catacombs, where many early Christian martyrs were buried, and made them places of pilgrimage. He wrote inscriptions for the principal shrines and churches to make pilgrims aware of their religious heritage. At the baptistry of St. John Lateran, where Roman Christians were baptized, Damasus wrote:

The multitude born here to live in heaven
*   has life from water and the life-giving Spirit.*
Sinner, seek the cleansing of this stream
*   that takes away the old and gives new life back.*

Nothing can divide where life unites,
*   one faith, one fount, one Spirit . . .*

The stream that flows below sprang from the
*   wounded Christ to wash the whole world.*

Children of the water, think no more of earth,
*   heaven will give you joy, in heaven is your hope.*

Damasus died at Rome on December 11, 384. He was buried with his mother and sister at a small church on the Via Ardeatina. At the cemetery of St. Callistus, his humble epitaph stated:

"I, Damasus, wished to be buried here but I feared to offend the ashes of these holy ones!"

Lord,
St. Damasus honored your martyrs so we may
continue to celebrate their witness for you.

OUR LADY OF GUADALUPE

ON DECEMBER 9, 1531, ten years after the Spanish conquest of Mexico, the Blessed Virgin appeared on the Tepeyac hill, then three miles from Mexico City, to Juan Diego, an Indian convert who was on his way to catechetcal instructions. She told him she wished a shrine to be built there. When Juan Diego told Bishop Zumarraga what had happened, he refused to believe him and asked for a sign.

Three days later, on December 12, the Blessed Mother appeared again to Juan and told him to gather in his coarsely woven cloak, roses which she arranged. When they were presented to Bishop Zumarraga he saw a picture of Our Lady of Guadalupe impressed on the cloak. The shrine at Guadalupe, where the picture is kept, was built in 1709 and is one of the great Marian shrines in the world and a national treasure for the Mexican people.

The hill of Tepeyac had a special meaning for the Indian people. A temple dedicated to the mother of a pagan god once stood there. The appearance of Mary dressed in their own clothing was a powerful incentive in the conversion of the native people to Christianity.

Pope Pius XII declared Our Lady of Guadalupe the patroness of the Americas.

Hail Mary, full of grace,
pray for us sinners.

ST. JANE FRANCES DE CHANTAL (1572-1641) religious

ST. JANE FRANCES DE CHANTAL was born of a prominent family at Dijon, France, on January 28, 1572. She married Christopher de Rabutin, Baron de Chantal, in 1592 at the age of twenty. They had six children and enjoyed a happy marriage. When her husband died in a hunting accident after nine years of marriage in 1601, she became desolate and sought spiritual guidance in her grief.

In 1607, she met St. Francis de Sales who encouraged and advised her for many years. Their friendship was to endure until his death in 1622. Jane Frances had an eager impetuous spirit and was anxious to progress in holiness. Her longing for perfection often left her discontented with herself and impatient for quick success. "There is something in me," she wrote, "that has never felt satisfied, but I cannot tell you what it is." Jane learned patience and gentleness gradually as she gave herself to performing simple acts of kindness for others.

In 1610, Jane founded, with the support of Francis, the Congregation of the Visitation (Visitation Order) at Annency. With the help of Mary Favre, Charlotte de Bréchard, Anne Caste, and ten companions, she vowed to imitate the virtues of Mary's visit to Elizabeth and engage in works of mercy for the poor and the sick who suffered so much neglect at that time. Her community lived a life of prayer and activity. By the time of her death at Moulins on December 13, 1641, there were eighty houses of her order. Jane Frances was buried at Annency near Francis de Sales.

> *What is your will for me, O God.*
> *I await your plan.*
> *I want to live only for you*
> *and be guided by you always.*
> *Grant that your holy will be done in me.*
>
> St. Jane Frances de Chantal

ST. LUCY   December 13
(d. 304) virgin and martyr

ACCORDING TO legend, St. Lucy was a young woman born at Syracuse, Italy. One day she went to the shrine of St. Agatha in Catania with her mother, who suffered from uncontrolled bleeding. While praying at the shrine, Lucy's mother was cured. Lucy decided to give up her worldly goods to serve the poor, took a vow of virginity, and broke off her impending marriage to a young nobleman in order to give her life entirely to God.

Her suitor was incensed at her action and accused her before the Roman consul of being a Christian who would not honor the laws of the Empire.

Bravely confessing her faith, Lucy was sentenced to be tortured by fire and boiling oil. She was unmoved by the ordeal and showed no sign of weakness. "God has granted that I should bear these things in order to free the faithful from the fear of suffering," she said. Though a sword was thrust through her throat, the young girl lived till communion was brought to her for her final journey to heaven. She died during the persecution under Emperor Diocletian in 304.

I am the Lord's poor servant,
to him alone I offer all in sacrifice.
I have nothing left to give except myself.

St. Lucy

ST. JOHN OF THE CROSS December 14
(1542-1591) priest and doctor

ST. JOHN was born at Fontiveros, Old Castile, Spain, in 1542. He was sent to school at Medina del Campo, but soon was apprenticed to a weaver. In 1559, he went to work for the governor of the hospital of Medina. He attended the Jesuit college at Medina and showed great talent as a student in theology and philosophy. John entered the Carmelite Order in 1563 and was ordained to the priesthood in 1567.

John was at Medina to celebrate his first Mass when he met St. Teresa of Avila. She spoke to him of her plans to reform the Carmelite Order. Though he had considered leaving the Carmelites, John decided to follow the primitive Carmelite rule and to assist Teresa in her task of reform. In 1568, joined by four companions, John founded the Discaled Carmelites. He took the name John of the Cross and monasteries were established at Duruelo, Pastrana, Mancera and Alcalá.

John suffered many misunderstandings and jealousies from fellow religious, even to the point of being imprisoned for nine months at Toledo in 1577. He continued, however, to write and preach on spiritual matters and devoted much time to guiding others in the spiritual life. His great treatises on the progress of the soul on its journey to God, such as *Dark Night of the Soul, Spiritual Canticle* and *Living Flame of Love,* have influenced spiritual theology profoundly.

In *Dark Night of the Soul,* written while he was imprisoned at Toledo, John describes the path to holiness as a demanding journey that must be made in the dark night of faith. He explains the workings of God's grace in the soul and the difficulties that face beginners in the spiritual life. *Spiritual Canti-*

cle and *Living Flame of Love* treat the mystical union that develops between God and the soul as it progresses in love. His writings demonstrate John's remarkable knowledge of the spiritual life which he expresses in poetry as well as prose. He is recognized as a Doctor of the Church for his ability to guide people to a more perfect life.

John died at La Peñuela Monastery in Andalusia, Spain, on December 13, 1591, repeating the words of the psalmist as Jesus had done, "Into your hands, O Lord, I commend my spirit."

My God,
  you will not take away what you have given me
  in your only Son, Jesus Christ.
  In him you have given me all I could desire.
    and so I wait patiently for you.

St. John of the Cross

ST. PETER CANISIUS   December 21
(1521-1597) priest and doctor

ST. PETER was born at Nijmegen, Holland, in 1521 into a prominent political family. He studied Canon Law at Louvain and received his master of arts degree at Cologne University in 1540. In 1543, while attending a retreat given by Blessed Peter Faber at Mainz, he decided to enter the Jesuits.

After some years of prayer and study in Cologne,

Peter was ordained in 1546. He began a career of writing and preaching and went to the Council of Trent for two sessions as a delegate. He returned to Rome and was commissioned by St. Ignatius Loyola to teach in the first Jesuit school at Messina. In 1549, he went to Ingolstadt, Germany, at the request of Duke William IV of Bavaria. In 1552, King Ferdinand asked Peter to go to Vienna. Peter's mission in Germany was to labor for the Church in its struggle with the Reformation. He taught at universities in Ingolstadt and Vienna and his preaching caused a religious revival among the Catholic people. He founded a new college at Prague in 1556 and won the respect of both Catholics and Protestants. He lived in Augsburg from 1559 to 1565 as the Jesuit superior and directed the ministry of his community for the revival of Catholicism in southern Germany.

Peter was a prolific writer and his famous catechism, or *Summary of Christian Doctrine,* was published in 1555. He produced a number of well-known catechisms, theological writings, editions of the writings of early Church theologians, as well as controversial essays. He went to Fribourg, Switzerland, in 1580 to establish a university. Today, the University of Fribourg is the result of his efforts. Peter died at Fribourg on December 21, 1597, leaving behind a vast legacy of apostolic works for the Church he loved so dearly.

St. Peter Canisius has been called the "Second Apostle of Germany"—the first being St. Boniface. In his diary he recalled the first commission he received in Rome to go to labor among the German people: "You know, Lord, how strongly and how often you committed Germany to my care on that very day. I was to continue to be solicitous for it thereafter; I was to desire to live and die for it." St. Peter Canisius is a Doctor of the Church.

My Savior,
you told me to draw the waters of my salvation
from your wellsprings.
I am eager that the streams of faith, hope and
love should flow into me from you.

St. Peter Canisius

ST. JOHN OF KANTI   December 23
(1390-1473) priest

ST. JOHN OF KANTI, also known as St. John Cantius, was born at Kanti, Poland, on June 23, 1390. A learned, holy man, he studied at the University of Cracow and was ordained to the priesthood. He taught for many years at the University of Cracow, where his colleagues and students admired his scholarly integrity and simple faith.

His success as a preacher and teacher caused his associates to become jealous of him. As a result, he served for a time as a parish priest in the city of

Olkusz. Because of problems in the parish, he would soon return to Cracow to teach Sacred Scripture at the university for the remainder of his life.

John endured envy and misunderstanding from some colleagues who resented his holy life and intellectual gifts, but he remained faithful to his teaching and pastoral work. Unconcerned for his own needs, he gave all he had to others, especially the poor. Desiring to become a martyr, John made a pilgrimage to the Holy Land to preach amongst the Turks. During his lifetime, he made four pilgrimages to Rome on foot.

Pope Clement XIII praised his holy teacher after his death, "He gave a wonderful example to university professors, an inspiration of complete dedication to duty and to teaching. . . With his humility went a rare and childlike simplicity. Every day after his teaching he would go straight from the lecture hall to the church and spend hours in prayer before Christ in the Eucharist. The God in his heart and the God on his lips were one and the same God."

John died at Cracow on Christmas eve, 1473.

O God,
   may we grow in wisdom and love.

ST. STEPHEN   December 26
(d. 34) first martyr

FROM EARLY in the fourth century, the deacon
Stephen has been honored by the Catholic Church
on December 26, the day after Christ's birth. He is
the first martyr, dying for his faith in Jesus, born of
Mary. The story of his persecution and death
before the Sanhedrin is told vividly in the Acts of
the Apostles.

"As a deacon appointed by the apostles after
Pentecost, Stephen was a man filled with
grace and power, who worked great wonders
and signs among the people. Certain
members of the so-called 'Synagogue of
Roman Freedmen' (that is, the Jews from
Cyrene, Alexandria, Cicilia and Asia) would
undertake to engage Stephen in debate, but
they proved no match for the wisdom and
spirit with which he spoke.

"Those who listened to his words were
stung to the heart; they ground their teeth in
anger at him. Stephen meanwhile, filled with
the Holy Spirit, looked to the sky above and
saw the glory of God and Jesus standing at
God's right hand. 'Look!' he exclaimed, 'I see
an opening in the sky and the Son of Man
standing at God's right hand.' The onlookers
were shouting aloud, holding their hands over
their ears as they did so. Then they rushed at
him as one man, dragged him out of the city,

and began to stone him. The witnesses meanwhile were piling their cloaks at the feet of a young man named Saul. As Stephen was being stoned he could be heard praying, 'Lord Jesus, receive my spirit.'"

"The love that brought Christ from heaven to earth raised Stephen from earth to heaven," says St. Fulgentius. Stephen's love gave him courage before an angry mob and prompted him to pray like Jesus for his persecutors.

St. Stephen, St. John the Apostle, and the Holy Innocents, whose feasts occur on the following days of December, are seen as special companions of Jesus. They are examples of the different ways of martyrdom for Christ. Stephen voluntarily accepted death and was executed for his faith. John willed to die for Christ, but was not martyred. The Holy Innocents died for Christ without understanding what was happening to them.

Into your hands, O Lord, I commend my spirit.

to John

ST. JOHN THE APOSTLE   December 27
(d. 100) apostle and evangelist

ST. JOHN was born in Galilee, the son of Zebedee the fisherman. Along with his brother, St. James the Great, he was called by Jesus to be one of his closest disciples. He witnessed the Transfiguration on Mount Tabor and Jesus' agony in the Garden of Gethsemani. As the "disciple whom Jesus loved," John rested his head on the Lord's breast at the Last Supper and was the only one to stand with Mary beneath the cross on Calvary. Jesus committed John to his mother's care, "Woman, behold your son," and in turn gave Mary to him as his mother, "Son, behold your mother."

On Easter Sunday, John ran with Peter to see the empty tomb and believed that Christ was risen from the dead. After Pentecost, at the temple gate with Peter, he healed the cripple who sat begging alms. John was a founder of the Church at Jerusalem and after some years went to Ephesus in Asia Minor. Here, according to tradition, he lived with Mary till her death and authored the great Gospel and Epistles that bear his name.

Early sources say that because of his teaching he was banished to the island of Patmos for a time and there wrote down revelations from heaven in a book called *The Apocalypse* or *Revelations*. He opposed heretics who denied that Jesus was God and taught his followers the great commandment of love. St. Jerome writes that as an old man too weak to engage in any activity, he would repeat to those he met, "My little children, love one another." When someone asked him why he repeated these same words over and over, he replied, "Because it is the Lord's teaching, and if you keep it you do enough."

He died at Ephesus when he was about ninety-four years old.

This is what we proclaim to you:
what was from the beginning,
what we have heard,
what we have seen with our eyes,
what we have looked upon
            and our hands have touched—
we speak of the word of life.

1 Jn. 1

HOLY INNOCENTS December 28
martyrs

ACCORDING TO the Gospel of Matthew, King Herod ordered the slaughter of all infant boys under two years old in Bethlehem in order to destroy an opponent to his rule.

This is the account in Matthew's words:

After the Magi had left, the angel of the Lord suddenly appeared in a dream to Joseph with the command: "Get up, take the child and his mother, and flee to Egypt. Stay there until I tell you otherwise. Herod is searching for the child to destroy him." Joseph got up and took the child and his mother and left that night for Egypt. He stayed there until the death of Herod, to fulfill what the Lord had said through the prophet:

"Out of Egypt I have called my son."

Once Herod realized that he had been deceived by the astrologers, he became furious. He ordered the massacre of all the boys two years old and under in Bethlehem and its environs, making his calculations on the basis of the date he had learned from the astrologers. What was said through Jeremiah the prophet was then fulfilled:

"A cry was heard at Ramah,
 sobbing and loud lamentation:
Rachel bewailing her children;
 no comfort for her, since they are no more."

Lord,
 give us your life
 even before we understand.

ST. THOMAS BECKET   December 29
(1118-1170) bishop and martyr

ST. THOMAS BECKET was born at London, England, on December 21, 1118. He was the son of wealthy and prominent parents and studied with the canons regular at Merton in Surrey. Well educated and socially connected, he obtained a position in the house of Theobald, Archbishop of Canterbury, at the age of twenty-four. He became the protege of Theobald, who would promote him to positions of power in the Church. He was ordained deacon in 1154 and nominated Archdeacon of Canterbury by Theobald. In 1155, he was appointed Chancellor of England by King Henry II, who valued his friendship as well as his advice. Accumulating wealth and surrounded by a magnificent court, Thomas lived in the lavish style of a great prince.

After the death of Theobald in 1161, Thomas was nominated as Archbishop of Canterbury by Henry and elected as Archbishop in May, 1162. His friendship with Henry was damaged by a series of conflicts between the government and the Church. Henry wanted a submissive Church that he could control, while Thomas could not in good conscience allow the Church's freedom and rights to be compromised. He changed his lavish life style and began to pursue his religious duties more seriously. In 1164, Thomas refused to accept the Constitutions of Clarendon, which denied the clergy the right to trial by a Church court and the right of appeal to Rome. As a result, he was forced to escape to France.

He remained in exile in France for six years and returned to England in 1170. When Thomas returned to England, Henry in exasperation called for someone to rid him of this troublesome priest. Four of his knights went at once to the Cathedral of Canterbury where they murdered Thomas on December 29, 1170. His death shocked Europe, and in 1173, Thomas Becket was canonized by Pope Alexander III.

O God,
    give us strength to uphold what is right.

ST. SYLVESTER I   December 31
   (d. 335) pope

ST. SYLVESTER, the son of a Roman named Rufinus, was a native of Rome. In 314, he succeeded Miltiades as Pope and presided over the Roman Church for twenty-one years. His office coincided practically with that of the Emperor Constantine who first granted toleration to Christianity and then during his reign gave Christians privileges and positions of power throughout the Empire. Sylvester governed through this crucial period, although Constantine exercised a dominant role in the affairs of the Church, summoning councils, hearing the complaints of bishops, and participating in religious and theological discussions.

Through his delegates, Sylvester participated at the Council of Arles in 313, which condemned the Donatist heresy, and the Council of Nicaea in 325, which condemned Arius. While he was Pope, the great churches of St. Peter, St. Lawrence, St. Agnes, and the Lateran basilica and baptistry were built by Constantine. The Lateran palace was given to the Pope as an official residence.

Later medieval legends called *The Acts of Blessed Sylvester* picture the Pope baptizing Constantine, curing the Emperor's leprosy, and participating in the finding of the true Cross. Medieval documents, especially the so-called *Donation of Constantine*, list the privileges and lands given to the Pope by the Emperor. Though unauthentic, these documents had great influence on medieval thought and politics.

Sylvester died on December 31, 335, and was buried in the cemetery of Priscilla on the Salarian Way in Rome.

> *Lord Jesus Christ,*
> *you founded your Church*
> *on the apostles.*
> *May we always hear your voice in*
> *their successors.*

INDEX OF SAINTS

317

PRINTED IN BELGIUM BY

INTERNATIONAL BOOK PRODUCTION